Introduction

Welcome to the *Air Fryer Baking Cookbook,*
where you'll discover a world of sweet baking that will tantalise your
taste buds and redefine your expectations of what an air fryer can do.

This versatile kitchen appliance is not just for frying. It's a secret
weapon for baking up your favourite treats without all the hassle and
heat of a conventional oven. Whether you're a busy parent, a time-
strapped student, or just someone who loves the convenience of easy
and quick baking, the air fryer is sure to become your new best friend.

With this cookbook, you'll have access to a wide range of delicious
and easy-to-make recipes that are tailored for the air fryer. From
classic cakes and pies to inventive dessert twists, you'll find
everything you need to satisfy your sweet tooth.
So, dust off your air fryer and get ready to embark on a culinary
journey that will make your heart sing and your family and friends
beg for more. Let's get baking!

*We want to take a moment to ask for your understanding as we publish the
Air Fryer Baking Cookbook in black and white. Our decision was based on a
desire to protect the environment and optimise costs. We understand that
some of our customers may prefer a colour publication, and we apologise in
advance if this causes any disappointment.
We hope that our customers will continue to support us in the future. And
thank you for being a part of our community and helping us make a positive
impact in the world."*

KEEP IN MIND
When baking with an air fryer

- Preheat the air fryer before placing your baked goods inside. This helps to ensure even cooking and consistent results.

- Use the right type of pan or dish for the recipe. Air fryer baskets can be used for items that need to be flipped, while trays with solid bottoms are best for baked goods that don't need to be flipped.

- Reduce the baking time and temperature compared to traditional oven baking. Air fryers cook faster than ovens, so be sure to adjust your recipe accordingly.

- Check your baked goods frequently to avoid burning or overcooking. Air fryers can cook quickly, so set a timer and check your food regularly.

- Use parchment paper or non-stick spray to prevent sticking. This will make it easier to remove your baked goods from the air fryer basket or tray.

- Don't overcrowd the air fryer basket or tray. This can lead to uneven cooking and may result in undercooked or overcooked baked goods.

- Use the right amount of batter or dough for the recipe. Overfilling the basket or tray can cause the batter to spill over or result in dense, undercooked baked goods.

- Experiment with different recipes to find what works best in your air fryer. Not all recipes will turn out perfectly in an air fryer, so don't be afraid to try new things.

- Let your baked goods cool before removing them from the air fryer basket or tray. This will prevent them from falling apart or sticking to the surface.

- Clean your air fryer thoroughly after each use to prevent leftover food particles from affecting the taste or quality of your next batch of baked goods.

COMMON BAKING MEASUREMENTS

1 cup all-purpose flour	4.5 oz	127 g
1 cup granulated sugar	7.1 oz	200 g
1 cup unsifted powdered sugar	4.4 oz	125 g
1 cup packed brown sugar	7.75 oz	220 g
1 cup rolled oats	3 oz	85 g
1 cup vegetable oil	7.7 oz	218 g
1 cup milk	8 oz.	227 g
1 cup heavy cream	8.4 oz	238 g
1 cup butter	8 oz.	227 g
1 large egg (white + yolk)	1.7 oz	48 g

COOKING MEASUREMENT EQUIVALENTS

Measurement	Abbreviation	Equivalent
Teaspoon	tsp	5 ml
Dessertspoon	dsp	10 ml
Tablespoon	tbsp	15 ml
Fluid ounce	fl oz	28.4 ml
Cup	-	240 ml
Pint	pt	568 ml
Quart	qt	1.14 L
Gallon	gal	4.55 L
Ounce	oz	28 g
Pound	lb	454 g
Milliliter	ml	1/1000 L
Gram	g	1/1000 kg
Inch	in	2.54 cm

TEMPERATURE

Celsius	Fahrenheit
100°C	212°F
110°C	230°F
120°C	250°F
140°C	284°F
150°C	300°F
160°C	320°F
175°C	350°F
180°C	356°F
200°C	392°F
220°C	428°F
240°C	464°F

Table of Content

Muffins & Brownies Recipes

Donuts Recipes

Donuts Recipes

More

Eccles Cake

INGREDIENTS

- 225g all-purpose flour
- 125g unsalted butter, chilled and cubed
- 120ml cold water
- 200g currants
- 1/2 tsp salt
- 50g unsalted butter, melted
- 50g caster sugar
- 1 tsp ground cinnamon

 Cooking Time 12 Minutes   **Servings** 12-15

INSTRUCTION

1. In a mixing bowl, sift the flour and salt together.
2. Rub the chilled butter cubes into the flour mixture until it forms a breadcrumb-like texture.
3. Add the cold water gradually, mixing with a spatula, until the dough comes together.
4. Roll the dough out on a floured surface into a large rectangle shape.
5. Brush the melted butter over the dough, leaving a 2 cm border around the edges.
6. Mix the currants, caster sugar, and ground cinnamon together and spread it over the buttered dough.
7. Fold the edges of the dough over the currant mixture and seal them together.
8. Flip the dough over so that the sealed side is on the bottom.
9. Cut the dough into 6 equal pieces and flatten them slightly.
10. Place the Eccles Cakes in the air fryer basket and air fry for 10-12 minutes at 180°C.
11. Once the Eccles Cakes are cooked, remove them from the air fryer and let them cool for 5 minutes before serving.
12. Serve the Eccles Cakes warm with a cup of tea and enjoy!

Madeira Cake

INGREDIENTS

- 175g unsalted butter, softened
- 175g caster sugar
- 225g self-raising flour
- 50g plain flour
- 3 medium eggs
- Zest of 1 lemon
- 4 tbsp milk

 Cooking Time
12 Minutes

 Servings
6-8

INSTRUCTION

1. In a mixing bowl, cream the butter and caster sugar together until light and fluffy.
2. Beat in the eggs, one at a time, adding a spoonful of flour with each egg.
3. Sift in the remaining self-raising flour and plain flour, and gently fold in until fully incorporated.
4. Mix in the lemon zest and milk until a smooth batter forms.
5. Grease a 6-inch cake tin that fits in your air fryer and pour in the cake batter.
6. Place the cake tin in the air fryer basket and air fry for 25-30 minutes at 160°C.
7. Once the cake is cooked, remove it from the air fryer and let it cool in the tin for 10 minutes before removing.
8. Serve the Madeira cake sliced and lightly dusted with icing sugar, if desired.

Carrot Cake

INGREDIENTS

- 150g self-raising flour
- 1 tsp baking powder
- 150g light brown sugar
- 2 medium eggs
- 125ml vegetable oil
- 1/2 tsp ground cinnamon
- 1/2 tsp ground nutmeg
- 1/4 tsp salt
- 1 tsp vanilla extract
- 150g grated carrots
- 50g chopped walnuts
- Cream cheese frosting (optional)

 Cooking Time 12 Minutes   **Servings** 6-8

INSTRUCTION

1. In a mixing bowl, whisk together the flour, baking powder, cinnamon, nutmeg, and salt.
2. In a separate bowl, beat the brown sugar, eggs, vegetable oil, and vanilla extract until well combined.
3. Add the dry ingredients to the wet mixture and stir until just combined.
4. Fold in the grated carrots and chopped walnuts until evenly distributed.
5. Grease a 6-inch cake tin that fits in your air fryer and pour in the carrot cake mixture.
6. Place the cake tin in the air fryer basket and air fry for 20-25 minutes at 160°C.
7. Once the cake is cooked, remove it from the air fryer and let it cool in the tin for 5 minutes before removing.
8. If desired, frost the cake with cream cheese frosting before serving.

Victoria Sponge Cake

INGREDIENTS

- 200g caster sugar
- 200g unsalted butter, room temperature
- 2 tbsp milk
- 1/2 tsp vanilla extract
- 4 medium eggs
- 200g self-raising flour
- Strawberry jam, for filling
- Icing sugar, for dusting

 Cooking Time 12 Minutes   **Servings** 6-8

INSTRUCTION

1. In a mixing bowl, cream the sugar and butter together until light and fluffy.
2. Beat in the eggs, one at a time, adding a spoonful of flour with each egg.
3. Sift the remaining flour into the bowl and gently fold in until fully incorporated.
4. Mix in the milk and vanilla extract.
5. Grease a 7 inch cake tin that fits in your air fryer.
6. Pour the mixture into the cake tin and smooth the top with a spatula.
7. Place the cake tin in the air fryer basket and air fry for 18-20 minutes at 160°C.
8. Remove the cake from the air fryer and let it cool in the tin for 5 minutes before removing.
9. Once the cake is completely cool, slice it horizontally in half using a serrated knife.
10. Spread the strawberry jam over the bottom half of the cake.
11. Sandwich the other half of the cake on top and dust the top with icing sugar before serving.

Lemon Drizzle Cake

INGREDIENTS

- 175g butter, softened
- 175g self-raising flour
- 1 1/2 tsp baking powder
- 175g caster sugar
- 3 medium eggs
- 2 tbsp milk
- Zest of 1 lemon
- Juice of 1 1/2 lemons
- 85g granulated sugar

 Cooking Time
12 Minutes

 Servings
6-8

INSTRUCTION

1. In a mixing bowl, cream the butter and caster sugar together until light and fluffy.
2. Beat in the eggs, one at a time, adding a spoonful of flour with each egg to avoid curdling.
3. Sift in the remaining flour, baking powder and gently fold in until fully incorporated.
4. Mix in the milk and lemon zest.
5. Pour the batter into a greased and lined 6-inch cake tin that fits in your air fryer.
6. Place the cake tin in the air fryer basket and air fry for 18-20 minutes at 160°C.
7. While the cake is cooking, mix together the lemon juice and granulated sugar to create the drizzle.
8. Once the cake is cooked, remove it from the air fryer and pierce the surface all over with a skewer.
9. Pour the lemon drizzle over the cake and let it absorb for 10-15 minutes before slicing and serving.

Fruit Cake

INGREDIENTS

- 150g unsalted butter
- 1/2 tsp mixed spice
- 1/2 tsp ground cinnamon
- 400g dried mixed fruit
- 150g caster sugar
- 3 medium eggs
- 200g self-raising flour
- 80ml brandy or orange juice
- 2 tbsp apricot jam

 Cooking Time
12 Minutes

 Servings
6-8

INSTRUCTION

1. In a mixing bowl, cream the butter and caster sugar together until light and fluffy.
2. Beat in the eggs, one at a time, adding a spoonful of flour with each egg.
3. Sift in the remaining flour, mixed spice and ground cinnamon, and gently fold in until fully incorporated.
4. Mix in the dried mixed fruit and brandy or orange juice.
5. Grease a 6-inch cake tin that fits in your air fryer and line the base with parchment paper.
6. Spoon the cake batter into the prepared tin and level the surface.
7. Place the cake tin in the air fryer basket and air fry for 25-30 minutes at 160°C.
8. After the cake has been in the air fryer for 15 minutes, loosely cover the top with aluminium foil to prevent it from browning too quickly.
9. Once the cake is cooked, remove it from the air fryer and let it cool in the tin for 10 minutes before removing.
10. While the cake is still warm, brush the surface with apricot jam for a glossy finish.

Chocolate Fudge Cake

INGREDIENTS

For the Cake:
- 200g unsalted butter, softened
- 200g caster sugar
- 4 medium eggs
- 175g self-raising flour
- 50g cocoa powder
- 1 tsp baking powder
- 2 tbsp milk

For the Fudge Icing:
- 200g dark chocolate, chopped
- 200ml double cream
- 50g unsalted butter

 Cooking Time
12 Minutes **Servings**
6-8

INSTRUCTION

1. In a mixing bowl, cream the butter and caster sugar together until light and fluffy.
2. Beat in the eggs, one at a time, adding a spoonful of flour with each egg.
3. Sift in the remaining flour, cocoa powder and baking powder, and gently fold in until fully incorporated.
4. Mix in the milk until a smooth batter forms.
5. Grease a 6-inch cake tin that fits in your air fryer and pour in the cake batter.
6. Place the cake tin in the air fryer basket and air fry for 20-25 minutes at 160°C.
7. While the cake is cooking, make the fudge icing. In a heatproof bowl, melt the chocolate, cream, and butter together in the microwave or over a pan of simmering water until smooth.
8. Once the cake is cooked, remove it from the air fryer and let it cool in the tin for 10 minutes before removing.
9. Spread the fudge icing over the cooled cake.

Coffee and Walnut Cake

INGREDIENTS

For the Cake:
- 175g unsalted butter, softened
- 175g caster sugar
- 3 medium eggs
- 175g self-raising flour
- 1 tsp baking powder
- 1 tbsp instant coffee granules, dissolved in 1 tbsp boiling water
- 50g chopped walnuts

For the Icing:
- 225g icing sugar
- 100g unsalted butter, softened
- 1 tbsp instant coffee granules, dissolved in 1 tbsp boiling water
- 50g chopped walnuts

 **Cooking Time**
12 Minutes

 Servings
6-8

INSTRUCTION

1. In a mixing bowl, cream the butter and caster sugar together until light and fluffy.
2. Beat in the eggs, one at a time, adding a spoonful of flour with each egg.
3. Sift in the remaining self-raising flour and baking powder, and gently fold in until fully incorporated.
4. Mix in the dissolved coffee and chopped walnuts until a smooth batter forms.
5. Grease a 6-inch cake tin that fits in your air fryer and pour in the cake batter.
6. Place the cake tin in the air fryer basket and air fry for 25-30 minutes at 160°C.
7. While the cake is cooking, make the icing. In a mixing bowl, beat the icing sugar and softened butter together until smooth.
8. Mix in the dissolved coffee and chopped walnuts until well combined.
9. Once the cake is cooked, remove it from the air fryer and let it cool in the tin for 10 minutes before removing.
10. Spread the coffee and walnut icing over the cooled cake.

Ginger Cake

INGREDIENTS

- 225g self-raising flour
- 1/2 tsp ground nutmeg
- 1/2 tsp baking soda
- 2 tsp ground ginger
- 1 tsp ground cinnamon
- 100g unsalted butter, softened
- 100g dark muscovado sugar
- 4 tbsp black treacle
- 2 medium eggs
- 150ml milk

 Cooking Time
12 Minutes

 Servings
8

INSTRUCTION

1. In a mixing bowl, sift together the self-raising flour, ground ginger, cinnamon, nutmeg, and baking soda.
2. In a separate mixing bowl, cream the butter, dark muscovado sugar, and black treacle together until light and fluffy.
3. Beat in the eggs, one at a time, adding a spoonful of the flour mixture with each egg.
4. Fold in the remaining flour mixture and milk, alternately, until fully incorporated.
5. Grease a 6-inch cake tin that fits in your air fryer and pour in the cake batter.
6. Place the cake tin in the air fryer basket and air fry for 25-30 minutes at 160°C.
7. Once the cake is cooked, remove it from the air fryer and let it cool in the tin for 10 minutes before removing.
8. Serve the Ginger Cake by slicing it into equal portions and enjoy!

Red Velvet Cake

INGREDIENTS

For the Cake:
- 125g unsalted butter, softened
- 225g caster sugar
- 2 large eggs, room temperature
- 1 tsp vanilla extract
- 2 tbsp cocoa powder
- 2 tbsp red food coloring
- 1 tsp baking soda
- 1/2 tsp salt
- 250g plain flour
- 240ml buttermilk

For the Cream Cheese Frosting:
- 200g cream cheese, room temperature
- 50g unsalted butter, softened
- 225g icing sugar
- 1 tsp vanilla extract

INSTRUCTION

1. In a mixing bowl, cream the butter and caster sugar together until light and fluffy.
2. Beat in the eggs, one at a time, adding a spoonful of flour with each egg.
3. Mix in the vanilla extract, cocoa powder, and red food coloring, until well combined.
4. Sift in the remaining flour, baking soda and salt, and fold in until fully incorporated.
5. Add the buttermilk gradually, mixing with a spatula, until a smooth cake batter forms.
6. Grease a 6-inch round cake tin that fits in your air fryer and pour in the cake batter.
7. Place the cake tin in the air fryer basket and air fry for 25-30 minutes at 160°C.
8. While the cake is cooking, make the cream cheese frosting. In a mixing bowl, beat the cream cheese, softened butter, icing sugar, and vanilla extract together until smooth.
9. Once the cake is cooked, remove it from the air fryer and let it cool in the tin for 10 minutes before removing.
10. Once cooled, spread the cream cheese frosting on top of the cake.

Apple Pie

INGREDIENTS

- 6 medium-sized apples, peeled, cored and thinly sliced (about 800g)
- 100g granulated sugar
- 1/2 teaspoon ground cinnamon
- 1/4 teaspoon ground nutmeg
- 1/4 teaspoon salt
- 1 tablespoon lemon juice
- 1 tablespoon cornstarch
- 1 sheet pre-made pie crust
- 1 egg, beaten
- 1 tablespoon coarse sugar

 Cooking Time 20 Minutes   **Servings** 8

INSTRUCTION

1. In a large bowl, mix together the sliced apples, granulated sugar, cinnamon, nutmeg, salt, lemon juice, and cornstarch until well combined.
2. Roll out the pre-made pie crust and cut into 8 equal slices.
3. Place a slice of pie crust into each of the wells in your air fryer basket.
4. Divide the apple mixture evenly between each of the wells, filling them to the top.
5. Take another slice of pie crust and lay it on top of the apples, pinching the edges of the crust together to seal.
6. Brush the beaten egg over the top of each pie.
7. Sprinkle the coarse sugar over the top of the egg wash.
8. Place the air fryer basket into the air fryer, set the temperature to 180°C, and set the timer for 15-20 minutes, until the crust is golden brown and the apples are cooked through.
9. Once the pies are done, remove them from the air fryer and let them cool for a few minutes before serving.

Cherry Pie

INGREDIENTS

- 500g frozen or fresh cherries, pitted
- 100g granulated sugar
- 3 tablespoons cornstarch
- 1/4 teaspoon salt
- 1/2 teaspoon almond extract
- 1 sheet pre-made pie crust
- 1 egg, beaten
- 1 tablespoon coarse sugar

 Cooking Time 20 Minutes   **Servings** 8

INSTRUCTION

1. In a medium-sized saucepan, mix together the cherries, granulated sugar, cornstarch, salt, and almond extract until well combined. Cook over medium heat for 5-7 minutes, stirring frequently, until the mixture has thickened and the cherries have released their juices. Remove from heat and let cool for a few minutes.
2. Roll out the pre-made pie crust and cut into 8 equal slices.
3. Place a slice of pie crust into each of the wells in your air fryer basket.
4. Divide the cherry mixture evenly between each of the wells, filling them to the top.
5. Take another slice of pie crust and lay it on top of the cherry filling, pinching the edges of the crust together to seal.
6. Brush the beaten egg over the top of each pie.
7. Sprinkle the coarse sugar over the top of the egg wash.
8. Place the air fryer basket into the air fryer, set the temperature to 180°C, and set the timer for 15-20 minutes, until the crust is golden brown and the cherry filling is bubbling.
9. Once the pies are done, remove them from the air fryer and let them cool for a few minutes before serving.

Blueberry Pie

INGREDIENTS

- 500g fresh blueberries
- 100g granulated sugar
- 2 tablespoons cornstarch
- 1 tablespoon lemon juice
- 1/4 teaspoon salt
- 1 sheet pre-made pie crust
- 1 egg, beaten
- 1 tablespoon coarse sugar

 Cooking Time
20 Minutes

 Servings
8

INSTRUCTION

1. In a medium-sized saucepan, mix together the blueberries, granulated sugar, cornstarch, lemon juice, and salt until well combined. Cook over medium heat for 5-7 minutes, stirring frequently, until the mixture has thickened and the blueberries have released their juices. Remove from heat and let cool for a few minutes.
2. Roll out the pre-made pie crust and cut into 8 equal slices.
3. Place a slice of pie crust into each of the wells in your air fryer basket.
4. Divide the blueberry mixture evenly between each of the wells, filling them to the top.
5. Take another slice of pie crust and lay it on top of the blueberry filling, pinching the edges of the crust together to seal.
6. Brush the beaten egg over the top of each pie.
7. Sprinkle the coarse sugar over the top of the egg wash.
8. Place the air fryer basket into the air fryer, set the temperature to 180°C, and set the timer for 15-20 minutes, until the crust is golden brown and the blueberry filling is bubbling.
9. Once the pies are done, remove them from the air fryer and let them cool for a few minutes before serving.

Peach Pie

INGREDIENTS

- 4-5 ripe peaches, peeled and sliced
- 100g granulated sugar
- 2 tablespoons cornstarch
- 1/2 teaspoon ground cinnamon
- 1/4 teaspoon ground nutmeg
- 1 sheet pre-made pie crust
- 1 egg, beaten
- 1 tablespoon coarse sugar

 **Cooking Time**
20 Minutes

 Servings
8

INSTRUCTION

1. In a medium-sized bowl, mix together the sliced peaches, granulated sugar, cornstarch, cinnamon, and nutmeg until well combined.
2. Roll out the pre-made pie crust and cut into 8 equal slices.
3. Place a slice of pie crust into each of the wells in your air fryer basket.
4. Divide the peach mixture evenly between each of the wells, filling them to the top.
5. Take another slice of pie crust and lay it on top of the peach filling, pinching the edges of the crust together to seal.
6. Brush the beaten egg over the top of each pie.
7. Sprinkle the coarse sugar over the top of the egg wash.
8. Place the air fryer basket into the air fryer, set the temperature to 180°C, and set the timer for 15-20 minutes, until the crust is golden brown and the peach filling is bubbling.
9. Once the pies are done, remove them from the air fryer and let them cool for a few minutes before serving.

Strawberry Rhubarb Pie

INGREDIENTS

- 1 pre-made pie crust
- 300g fresh rhubarb, chopped
- 250g fresh strawberries, hulled and sliced
- 100g granulated sugar
- 2 tablespoons cornstarch
- 1/2 teaspoon ground cinnamon
- 1/4 teaspoon ground ginger
- 1 egg, beaten
- 1 tablespoon coarse sugar

 Cooking Time 30 Minutes   **Servings** 8

INSTRUCTION

1. In a medium-sized bowl, mix together the chopped rhubarb, sliced strawberries, granulated sugar, cornstarch, cinnamon, and ginger until well combined.
2. Roll out the pre-made pie crust and place it into the bottom of your air fryer basket.
3. Pour the fruit mixture onto the pie crust.
4. Take another slice of pie crust and lay it on top of the fruit filling, pinching the edges of the crust together to seal.
5. Brush the beaten egg over the top of the pie.
6. Sprinkle the coarse sugar over the top of the egg wash.
7. Place the air fryer basket into the air fryer, set the temperature to 180°C, and set the timer for 25-30 minutes, until the crust is golden brown and the fruit filling is bubbling.
8. Once the pie is done, remove it from the air fryer and let it cool for a few minutes before serving.

Lemon Meringue Pie

 **Cooking Time**
12 Minutes

 Servings
8

INGREDIENTS

For the crust:

- 1 pre-made pie crust

For the filling:

- 4 large eggs, separated
- 200g granulated sugar
- 30g cornstarch
- 30g all-purpose flour
- 1/4 teaspoon salt
- 350ml water
- 120ml fresh lemon juice
- 30g unsalted butter
- 1 tablespoon grated lemon zest

For the meringue:

- 4 large egg whites
- 1/4 teaspoon cream of tartar
- 50g granulated sugar

INSTRUCTION

1. Preheat your air fryer to 375°F (190°C).
2. Roll out the pre-made pie crust and place it into the bottom of your pie dish.
3. In a medium-sized bowl, whisk together the egg yolks, granulated sugar, cornstarch, flour, and salt until well combined.
4. In a medium-sized saucepan, heat the water, lemon juice, butter, and lemon zest over medium heat until the butter is melted and the mixture is hot but not boiling.
5. Slowly pour the hot lemon mixture into the egg yolk mixture, whisking constantly, until well combined.
6. Pour the lemon mixture into the prepared pie crust.
7. In a large bowl, beat the egg whites and cream of tartar with an electric mixer until soft peaks form.
8. Gradually add the granulated sugar, beating constantly, until stiff peaks form.
9. Spoon the meringue over the top of the lemon filling, making sure to cover the edges of the crust.
10. Place the pie dish into the air fryer and cook for 10-12 minutes, until the meringue is golden brown.
11. Remove the pie from the air fryer and let it cool to room temperature before serving.

Key Lime Pie

INGREDIENTS

For the crust:
- 150g digestive biscuits
- 75g unsalted butter, melted
- For the filling:
- 4 large egg yolks
- 1 can (397g) sweetened condensed milk
- 120ml fresh lime juice
- 1 tablespoon lime zest

For the topping:
- 120ml double cream
- 1 tablespoon icing sugar
- Lime slices, for garnish (optional)

 **Cooking Time**
12 Minutes

 Servings
8

INSTRUCTION

1. Crush the digestive biscuits into fine crumbs using a food processor or by placing them in a resealable plastic bag and crushing with a rolling pin.
2. In a mixing bowl, combine the biscuit crumbs and melted butter until the mixture resembles wet sand.
3. Press the mixture into the bottom of a 9-inch pie dish.
4. In a separate bowl, whisk together the egg yolks, sweetened condensed milk, lime juice, and lime zest until well combined.
5. Pour the filling into the prepared pie crust.
6. Place the pie dish into the air fryer and cook at 175°C for 10-12 minutes, or until the filling is set.
7. Remove the pie from the air fryer and let it cool to room temperature.
8. In a separate mixing bowl, whip the double cream and icing sugar together until stiff peaks form.
9. Spread the whipped cream over the top of the cooled pie.
10. Garnish with lime slices, if desired.
11. Chill the pie in the refrigerator for at least 2 hours before serving.

Pecan Pie

INGREDIENTS

For the crust:

- 250g plain flour
- 1 tablespoon caster sugar
- 1/2 teaspoon salt
- 120g unsalted butter, chilled and cubed
- 1 egg yolk
- 2-3 tablespoons cold water

For the filling:

- 3 large eggs
- 175g golden syrup
- 75g light brown sugar
- 75g unsalted butter, melted
- 1 teaspoon vanilla extract
- 200g pecans, chopped

 **Cooking Time** 25 Minutes   **Servings** 8

INSTRUCTION

1. In a mixing bowl, combine the plain flour, caster sugar, and salt. Add the chilled butter and use your fingers to rub the butter into the flour mixture until it resembles breadcrumbs.
2. Mix in the egg yolk and enough cold water to bring the dough together into a ball.
3. Roll out the dough on a floured surface and transfer it to a 9-inch pie dish.
4. In a separate mixing bowl, whisk together the eggs, golden syrup, light brown sugar, melted butter, and vanilla extract until well combined.
5. Stir in the chopped pecans.
6. Pour the filling into the prepared pie crust.
7. Place the pie dish into the air fryer and cook at 175°C for 20-25 minutes, or until the filling is set and the crust is golden brown.
8. Remove the pie from the air fryer and let it cool to room temperature.
9. Serve with whipped cream or ice cream, if desired.

Chocolate Cream Pie

INGREDIENTS

For the crust:

- 200g digestive biscuits
- 100g unsalted butter, melted
- For the filling:
- 500ml double cream
- 150g milk chocolate, chopped
- 150g dark chocolate, chopped
- 2 tablespoons caster sugar
- 2 teaspoons vanilla extract

For the topping:

- 150ml double cream
- 1 tablespoon icing sugar
- Chocolate shavings, for garnish

 Cooking Time 7 Minutes   Servings 8

INSTRUCTION

1. Crush the digestive biscuits in a plastic bag with a rolling pin or pulse in a food processor until they form fine crumbs.
2. Mix the melted butter with the biscuit crumbs until fully combined. Press the mixture into a 9-inch pie dish, pressing down firmly and evenly.
3. Chill the crust in the refrigerator while you prepare the filling.
4. In a saucepan, heat the double cream, chopped milk chocolate, chopped dark chocolate, caster sugar, and vanilla extract over low heat, stirring constantly until the chocolate has melted and the mixture is smooth and well combined.
5. Pour the chocolate mixture into the prepared crust and smooth the top with a spatula. Chill in the refrigerator for at least 2 hours or until set.
6. To make the topping, whip the double cream and icing sugar together until stiff peaks form.
7. Spread the whipped cream over the chilled chocolate filling and sprinkle with chocolate shavings.
8. Place the pie dish into the air fryer and cook at 160°C for 5-7 minutes or until the whipped cream topping is lightly browned.
9. Remove the pie from the air fryer and let it cool to room temperature before serving.

Lavender Cookies

INGREDIENTS

- 200g all-purpose flour
- 100g unsalted butter, softened
- 100g caster sugar
- 1 large egg
- 1 tsp baking powder
- 2 tbsp dried culinary lavender
- Pinch of salt

 Cooking Time 12 Minutes   **Servings** 12-15

INSTRUCTION

1. In a mixing bowl, cream together the butter and caster sugar until light and fluffy.
2. Add in the egg and mix until fully incorporated.
3. In a separate bowl, mix together the flour, baking powder, lavender, and salt.
4. Gradually add the dry ingredients to the wet mixture, mixing until a dough forms.
5. Form the dough into a ball and wrap it in cling film. Chill in the fridge for at least 30 minutes.
6. Preheat the air fryer to 160°C.
7. Remove the dough from the fridge and roll it out on a floured surface until it's about 1/4 inch thick.
8. Use a cookie cutter to cut out your desired shapes and place them onto a baking tray lined with parchment paper.
9. Place the tray into the air fryer and cook for 10-12 minutes, until the cookies are lightly golden.
10. Remove the cookies from the air fryer and allow them to cool on a wire rack.

Rosemary Cookies

INGREDIENTS

- 225g unsalted butter, softened
- 150g granulated sugar
- 1 large egg yolk
- 1 tsp vanilla extract
- 300g plain flour
- 2 tbsp fresh rosemary, chopped
- 1/4 tsp salt

 Cooking Time
10 Minutes

 Servings
24-30

INSTRUCTION

1. In a large bowl, beat the softened butter and granulated sugar together until light and fluffy.
2. Beat in the egg yolk and vanilla extract.
3. In a separate bowl, whisk together the plain flour, chopped rosemary, and salt.
4. Gradually add the dry mixture to the butter mixture, stirring until a dough forms.
5. Divide the dough into two equal portions, then roll each portion into a log about 2 inches in diameter.
6. Wrap each log in plastic wrap and chill in the fridge for at least 30 minutes.
7. Preheat the air fryer to 175°C.
8. Slice the chilled dough logs into 1/4 inch thick rounds and place them on a baking sheet lined with parchment paper.
9. Cook the cookies in the air fryer for 8-10 minutes or until the edges are lightly golden.
10. Let the cookies cool on the baking sheet for 5 minutes before transferring them to a wire rack to cool completely.

Sesame Cookies

INGREDIENTS

- 110g unsalted butter, at room temperature
- 90g caster sugar
- 1 large egg
- 1 tsp vanilla extract
- 210g plain flour
- 1 tsp baking powder
- 1/4 tsp salt
- 50g sesame seeds

 Cooking Time
10 Minutes

 Servings
20

INSTRUCTION

1. In a mixing bowl, cream together the butter and caster sugar until light and fluffy.
2. Beat in the egg and vanilla extract.
3. In a separate bowl, whisk together the flour, baking powder, and salt.
4. Gradually stir the dry ingredients into the butter mixture until a dough forms.
5. Shape the dough into a log and wrap it in cling film. Refrigerate for at least 30 minutes.
6. Preheat the air fryer to 170°C.
7. Cut the dough into thin slices and arrange them on a lined baking sheet.
8. Sprinkle the sesame seeds over the cookies, pressing them down lightly to adhere.
9. Bake in the air fryer for 8-10 minutes or until golden brown.
10. Allow the cookies to cool on the baking sheet for 5 minutes before transferring to a wire rack to cool completely.
11. Store the cookies in an airtight container for up to 1 week.

Pecan Cookies

INGREDIENTS

- 200g plain flour
- 115g unsalted butter, softened
- 90g light brown sugar
- 1 large egg
- 1 tsp vanilla extract
- 1/2 tsp baking powder
- 1/4 tsp salt
- 80g pecans, chopped
- Extra pecan halves for decoration.

 Cooking Time 12 Minutes   **Servings** 12-14

INSTRUCTION

1. In a medium bowl, whisk together the flour, baking powder, and salt.
2. In a separate bowl, beat the butter and brown sugar until light and fluffy.
3. Beat in the egg and vanilla extract.
4. Gradually add the flour mixture to the butter mixture, mixing until just combined.
5. Stir in the chopped pecans.
6. Divide the dough into 12-14 balls and flatten slightly.
7. Place the dough balls in the air fryer basket, leaving some space between each cookie.
8. Place a pecan half on top of each cookie for decoration.
9. Air fry the cookies at 160°C for 10-12 minutes, or until the edges are golden brown.
10. Allow the cookies to cool on a wire rack before serving.

Pistachio Cookies

INGREDIENTS

- 150g unsalted butter, at room temperature
- 100g caster sugar
- 1 large egg, at room temperature
- 1/2 tsp vanilla extract
- 200g plain flour
- 1/4 tsp salt
- 100g shelled pistachios, chopped

 Cooking Time 10 Minutes

 Servings 16-18

INSTRUCTION

1. In a large mixing bowl, cream the butter and sugar together until light and fluffy.
2. Add the egg and vanilla extract to the mixing bowl and mix until well combined.
3. In a separate mixing bowl, whisk together the flour and salt.
4. Gradually add the flour mixture to the butter mixture, mixing until just combined.
5. Fold in the chopped pistachios.
6. Preheat your air fryer to 160°C.
7. Line your air fryer basket with parchment paper.
8. Scoop spoonfuls of the cookie dough onto the parchment paper, spacing them 1 inch apart.
9. Gently press down on the dough to slightly flatten each cookie.
10. Air fry the cookies for 8-10 minutes, or until lightly golden brown.
11. Remove the cookies from the air fryer and let them cool on a wire rack before serving.

Walnut Cookies

INGREDIENTS

- 150g unsalted butter, at room temperature
- 80g caster sugar
- 1 egg yolk
- 200g plain flour
- 1/4 teaspoon salt
- 50g chopped walnuts
- Extra caster sugar for sprinkling

 **Cooking Time**
10 Minutes

 Servings
16-20

INSTRUCTION

1. In a mixing bowl, cream together the butter and sugar until light and fluffy.
2. Beat in the egg yolk until well combined.
3. Add the flour and salt and mix until a dough forms.
4. Fold in the chopped walnuts.
5. Roll the dough into a log and wrap in cling film. Chill for at least 30 minutes.
6. Preheat the air fryer at 160°C for 5 minutes.
7. Slice the dough into 1cm thick rounds and place on a baking tray lined with parchment paper.
8. Sprinkle a little caster sugar over each cookie.
9. Place the tray in the air fryer basket and bake for 8-10 minutes or until golden brown.
10. Remove from the air fryer and allow to cool on the tray for 5 minutes, then transfer to a wire rack to cool completely.

Molasses Cookies

INGREDIENTS

- 220g all-purpose flour
- 1 tsp baking powder
- 1/2 tsp baking soda
- 1 1/2 tsp ground ginger
- 1 tsp ground cinnamon
- 1/4 tsp ground nutmeg
- 1/4 tsp salt
- 1 egg
- 115g unsalted butter, room temperature
- 100g granulated sugar
- 50g dark molasses
- 1 tsp vanilla extract

 Cooking Time
10 Minutes

 Servings
24

INSTRUCTION

1. In a mixing bowl, whisk together the flour, baking powder, baking soda, ginger, cinnamon, nutmeg, and salt.
2. In a separate bowl, beat the butter with the sugar until light and fluffy.
3. Mix in the molasses, egg, and vanilla extract until well combined.
4. Add the dry ingredients to the wet mixture and stir until a dough forms.
5. Cover the dough with plastic wrap and refrigerate for at least 30 minutes or overnight.
6. Preheat your air fryer to 180°C.
7. Roll the dough into 1 inch balls and place them on a greased air fryer basket.
8. Flatten each ball slightly with the back of a fork.
9. Air fry the cookies for 8 to 10 minutes or until light golden brown.
10. Let the cookies cool on the basket for 5 minutes before transferring them to a wire rack to cool completely.

Gingersnap Cookies

INGREDIENTS

- 200g all-purpose flour
- 1 tsp baking soda
- 1 1/4 tsp ground ginger
- 1 tsp ground cinnamon
- 1/4 tsp salt
- 115g unsalted butter, room temperature
- 150g granulated sugar, plus extra for rolling
- 1 egg
- 3 tbsp golden syrup

 Cooking Time
10 Minutes

 Servings
24

INSTRUCTION

1. In a mixing bowl, whisk together the flour, baking soda, ginger, cinnamon, and salt.
2. In a separate bowl, beat the butter with the sugar until light and fluffy.
3. Mix in the egg and golden syrup until well combined.
4. Add the dry ingredients to the wet mixture and stir until a dough forms.
5. Cover the dough with plastic wrap and refrigerate for at least 30 minutes or overnight.
6. Preheat your air fryer to 175°C.
7. Roll the dough into 1 inch balls and coat each ball in granulated sugar.
8. Place the balls on a greased air fryer basket, leaving space between them.
9. Air fry the cookies for 6 to 8 minutes or until set and slightly cracked.
10. Let the cookies cool on the basket for 5 minutes before transferring them to a wire rack to cool completely.

Orange Cookies

INGREDIENTS

- 150g all-purpose flour
- 1/2 tsp baking powder
- 1/4 tsp salt
- 1 tbsp fresh orange juice
- 1/4 tsp vanilla extract
- 75g unsalted butter, room temperature
- 100g granulated sugar
- 1 egg
- 1 tbsp orange zest
- 50g powdered sugar

 Cooking Time
10 Minutes

 Servings
16

INSTRUCTION

1. In a mixing bowl, whisk together the flour, baking powder, and salt.
2. In a separate bowl, beat the butter and granulated sugar until light and fluffy.
3. Mix in the egg, orange zest, orange juice, and vanilla extract until well combined.
4. Add the dry ingredients to the wet mixture and stir until a dough forms.
5. Cover the dough with plastic wrap and refrigerate for at least 30 minutes.
6. Preheat your air fryer to 175°C. Line the air fryer basket with parchment paper.
7. Roll the dough into 1-inch balls and place them on the parchment-lined air fryer basket. Flatten each ball slightly with the back of a fork.
8. Air fry the cookies for 8-10 minutes or until the edges are lightly golden brown and the cookies are set.
9. Remove the cookies from the air fryer and let them cool on the basket for 5 minutes.
10. In a small bowl, whisk together the powdered sugar and enough orange juice to make a smooth and drizzly glaze. Drizzle the glaze over the cookies and let it set before serving.

Cranberry Cookies

INGREDIENTS

- 200g all-purpose flour
- 1 tsp baking powder
- 1/2 tsp baking soda
- 1 egg
- 1 tsp vanilla extract
- 1/4 tsp salt
- 115g unsalted butter, room temperature
- 100g granulated sugar
- 100g dried cranberries

 Cooking Time 10 Minutes   **Servings** 16-20

INSTRUCTION

1. In a mixing bowl, whisk together the flour, baking powder, baking soda, and salt.
2. In a separate bowl, beat the butter with the sugar until light and fluffy.
3. Mix in the egg and vanilla extract until well combined.
4. Add the dry ingredients to the wet mixture and stir until a dough forms.
5. Fold in the cranberries.
6. Cover the dough with plastic wrap and refrigerate for at least 30 minutes or overnight.
7. Preheat your air fryer to 175°C.
8. Roll the dough into 1 inch balls and place them on a greased air fryer basket, leaving space between them.
9. Flatten each ball slightly with the back of a fork.
10. Air fry the cookies for 8 to 10 minutes or until lightly golden brown.
11. Let the cookies cool on the basket for 5 minutes before transferring them to a wire rack to cool completely.

Chocolate Chip Cookies

INGREDIENTS

- 115g unsalted butter, softened
- 100g granulated sugar
- 100g light brown sugar
- 1 large egg
- 1 tsp vanilla extract
- 225g all-purpose flour
- 1 tsp baking soda
- 1/2 tsp salt
- 150g chocolate chips

 Cooking Time
10 Minutes

 Servings
20-24

INSTRUCTION

1. In a large bowl, cream together the butter, granulated sugar, and light brown sugar until light and fluffy.
2. Add in the egg and vanilla extract, and mix until well combined.
3. In a separate bowl, whisk together the flour, baking soda, and salt.
4. Add the dry ingredients to the wet mixture and mix until just combined.
5. Fold in the chocolate chips.
6. Cover the bowl with cling film and chill the dough in the refrigerator for at least 30 minutes.
7. Preheat the air fryer to 170°C.
8. Form the dough into small balls, about 1 tablespoon each, and place them onto the air fryer basket.
9. Cook the cookies in the air fryer for 8-10 minutes or until golden brown.
10. Remove from the air fryer and allow to cool on a wire rack.

Oatmeal Raisin Cookies

INGREDIENTS

- 115g unsalted butter, softened
- 100g brown sugar
- 50g granulated sugar
- 1 large egg
- 1 tsp vanilla extract
- 120g all-purpose flour
- 1 tsp cinnamon
- 1/2 tsp baking soda
- 1/4 tsp salt
- 135g old-fashioned oats
- 150g raisins

 Cooking Time
10 Minutes   **Servings**
18-20

INSTRUCTION

1. In a large mixing bowl, cream together the softened butter, brown sugar, and granulated sugar until light and fluffy.
2. Add the egg and vanilla extract to the mixture and beat until well combined.
3. In a separate bowl, whisk together the flour, cinnamon, baking soda, and salt. Add this mixture to the butter mixture and stir until just combined.
4. Fold in the oats and raisins until evenly distributed throughout the dough.
5. Using a small cookie scoop or spoon, drop the dough by rounded tablespoons onto a greased air fryer basket or tray, leaving some space between each cookie.
6. Air fry the cookies at 180°C for 8-10 minutes or until the edges are golden brown and the centers are set.
7. Remove the cookies from the air fryer and allow them to cool on a wire rack before serving.

Peanut Butter Cookies

INGREDIENTS

- 125g unsalted butter, softened
- 125g caster sugar
- 125g crunchy peanut butter
- 1 large egg, beaten
- 200g plain flour
- 1/2 tsp baking powder
- 1/2 tsp bicarbonate of soda
- Pinch of salt

 Cooking Time 10 Minutes   **Servings** 12-14

INSTRUCTION

1. In a mixing bowl, cream the butter and caster sugar together until light and fluffy.
2. Beat in the peanut butter and egg until well combined.
3. In a separate bowl, mix together the flour, baking powder, bicarbonate of soda, and salt.
4. Gradually add the dry ingredients to the wet ingredients and mix until a dough forms.
5. Roll the dough into small balls, about 1 tablespoon each, and place them onto a lined air fryer basket, making sure to leave some space between them.
6. Flatten the balls slightly with the back of a fork.
7. Set the air fryer to 160°C and cook the cookies for 8-10 minutes, or until they're golden brown and firm to the touch.
8. Let the cookies cool on the air fryer basket for a few minutes before transferring them to a wire rack to cool completely.
9. Serve and enjoy your peanut butter cookies!

Shortbread Cookies

INGREDIENTS

- 200g plain flour
- 100g cornflour
- 100g caster sugar
- 225g unsalted butter, at room temperature
- Pinch of salt

 Cooking Time
12 Minutes

 Servings
18-20

INSTRUCTION

1. In a mixing bowl, cream together the butter and sugar until light and fluffy.
2. In a separate bowl, whisk together the plain flour, cornflour, and salt.
3. Gradually add the dry mixture to the creamed butter mixture, mixing until a smooth dough forms.
4. Roll out the dough on a floured surface until it is approximately 1cm thick.
5. Cut the dough into your desired shapes and place them onto a piece of baking paper.
6. Place the baking paper with the cut-out cookies into the air fryer basket.
7. Set the air fryer to 160°C and cook for 10-12 minutes.
8. Once the cookies are done, remove the basket from the air fryer and allow the cookies to cool for a few minutes before transferring them to a wire rack to cool completely.

Snickerdoodle Cookies

INGREDIENTS

- 175g unsalted butter, softened
- 150g granulated sugar
- 1 large egg
- 1 tsp vanilla extract
- 250g plain flour
- 1/2 tsp baking powder
- 1/2 tsp salt
- 1 tsp ground cinnamon
- 25g granulated sugar, for rolling
- 1 tsp ground cinnamon, for rolling.

 Cooking Time 10 Minutes   **Servings** 12

INSTRUCTION

1. In a large mixing bowl, cream together the butter and sugar until light and fluffy.
2. Add the egg and vanilla extract and mix well.
3. In a separate bowl, whisk together the flour, baking powder, salt, and cinnamon.
4. Gradually add the dry ingredients to the butter mixture, mixing until just combined.
5. Cover the bowl with plastic wrap and refrigerate the dough for at least 30 minutes.
6. In a small bowl, mix together the remaining sugar and cinnamon.
7. Preheat the air fryer to 160°C .
8. Roll the dough into balls about 1 1/2 inches in diameter.
9. Roll each ball in the cinnamon sugar mixture to coat it completely.
10. Place the balls in the air fryer basket, making sure to leave some space between them.
11. Cook the cookies for 8-10 minutes, until they are lightly golden brown.
12. Remove the cookies from the air fryer and allow them to cool on a wire rack before serving.

Gingerbread Cookies

INGREDIENTS

- 150g unsalted butter, softened
- 150g dark brown sugar
- 1 large egg
- 75g black treacle
- 375g plain flour
- 1 1/2 tsp baking powder
- 2 tsp ground ginger
- 1 tsp ground cinnamon
- 1/2 tsp ground nutmeg
- 1/2 tsp ground cloves
- 1/2 tsp salt

 Cooking Time 10 Minutes   **Servings** 24-30

INSTRUCTION

1. In a large mixing bowl, cream the butter and sugar until light and fluffy.
2. Beat in the egg and treacle until well combined.
3. In a separate bowl, sift together the flour, baking powder, ginger, cinnamon, nutmeg, cloves, and salt.
4. Gradually add the dry ingredients to the wet mixture and mix until a dough forms.
5. Divide the dough into two equal portions, wrap each in clingfilm, and chill in the fridge for at least 30 minutes.
6. Preheat the air fryer to 180°C.
7. On a floured surface, roll out one portion of the dough to 1/4-inch thickness.
8. Use cookie cutters to cut out desired shapes and place them on a baking sheet lined with parchment paper.
9. Repeat with the second portion of dough.
10. Place the baking sheet in the air fryer and bake for 8-10 minutes, or until the edges are lightly browned.
11. Remove from the air fryer and allow to cool on the baking sheet for 5 minutes before transferring to a wire rack to cool completely. Serve and enjoy!

Sugar Cookies

INGREDIENTS

- 250g all-purpose flour
- 1/2 tsp baking powder
- 1/4 tsp salt
- 115g unsalted butter, room temperature
- 150g granulated sugar
- 1 egg
- 1 tsp vanilla extract

 Cooking Time
10 Minutes

 Servings
24

INSTRUCTION

1. In a mixing bowl, whisk together the flour, baking powder, and salt.
2. In a separate bowl, beat the butter with the sugar until light and fluffy.
3. Mix in the egg and vanilla extract until well combined.
4. Add the dry ingredients to the wet mixture and stir until a dough forms.
5. Cover the dough with plastic wrap and refrigerate for at least 30 minutes or overnight.
6. Preheat your air fryer to 175°C.
7. Roll the dough into 1 inch balls and place them on a greased air fryer basket, leaving space between them.
8. Flatten each ball slightly with the back of a fork.
9. Air fry the cookies for 6 to 8 minutes or until lightly golden brown.
10. Let the cookies cool on the basket for 5 minutes before transferring them to a wire rack to cool completely.

Toffee Cookies

INGREDIENTS

- 125g unsalted butter, softened
- 100g caster sugar
- 50g light brown sugar
- 1 large egg
- 1 tsp vanilla extract
- 225g self-raising flour
- 100g toffee pieces

 Cooking Time
10 Minutes

 Servings
16

INSTRUCTION

1. In a large mixing bowl, cream together the softened butter, caster sugar, and light brown sugar until light and fluffy.
2. Beat in the egg and vanilla extract until well combined.
3. Gradually add the self-raising flour, mixing until just combined.
4. Fold in the toffee pieces.
5. Form the dough into a ball, wrap in cling film and refrigerate for at least 30 minutes.
6. Preheat the air fryer to 180°C.
7. Remove the dough from the refrigerator and shape into small balls, about 1 tbsp each.
8. Place the cookie dough balls onto a piece of baking paper, leaving enough space between each one for spreading during cooking.
9. Place the baking paper into the air fryer basket and cook for 8-10 minutes, until the cookies are golden brown.
10. Remove from the air fryer basket and allow to cool on a wire rack.

Macadamia Nut Cookies

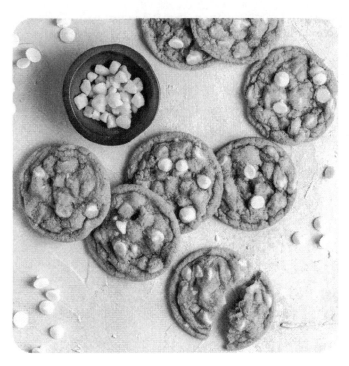

INGREDIENTS

- 150g unsalted butter, softened
- 75g caster sugar
- 75g brown sugar
- 1 large egg
- 1 tsp vanilla extract
- 225g self-raising flour
- 1/2 tsp baking powder
- 100g macadamia nuts, roughly chopped.

 Cooking Time 10 Minutes   **Servings** 20-24

INSTRUCTION

1. In a mixing bowl, cream the softened butter, caster sugar, and brown sugar until light and fluffy.
2. Add the egg and vanilla extract to the mixture, and beat well.
3. Sift in the self-raising flour and baking powder, and mix until well combined.
4. Fold in the chopped macadamia nuts.
5. Roll the dough into small balls, and place them onto a lined air fryer basket, leaving some space between each ball.
6. Gently flatten each ball with a fork.
7. Air fry the cookies at 160°C for 8-10 minutes or until golden brown.
8. Remove the cookies from the air fryer basket and let them cool on a wire rack.

Double Chocolate Cookies

INGREDIENTS

- 125g unsalted butter, softened
- 100g caster sugar
- 100g light brown sugar
- 1 large egg
- 1 tsp vanilla extract
- 150g plain flour
- 50g cocoa powder
- 1/2 tsp baking powder
- 1/2 tsp baking soda
- 1/2 tsp salt
- 100g chocolate chips

 Cooking Time
10 Minutes

 Servings
12-15

INSTRUCTION

1. Preheat your air fryer to 160°C.
2. In a bowl, cream together the butter, caster sugar, and brown sugar until light and fluffy.
3. Beat in the egg and vanilla extract until combined.
4. In another bowl, whisk together the flour, cocoa powder, baking powder, baking soda, and salt.
5. Gradually add the dry ingredients into the wet mixture until just combined.
6. Fold in the chocolate chips.
7. Roll the cookie dough into small balls and place them onto a lined air fryer basket.
8. Gently press down on the cookie balls to slightly flatten them.
9. Air fry the cookies for 8-10 minutes or until the edges are set and the centers are still slightly soft.
10. Let the cookies cool for a few minutes before serving. Enjoy!

S'mores Cookies

INGREDIENTS

- 150g plain flour
- 1 tsp baking powder
- 1/4 tsp salt
- 100g unsalted butter, softened
- 100g light brown sugar
- 1 egg, beaten
- 1 tsp vanilla extract
- 100g digestive biscuits, crushed
- 50g mini marshmallows
- 50g milk chocolate chips

 Cooking Time
12 Minutes

 Servings
8-10

INSTRUCTION

1. In a bowl, mix together the flour, baking powder, and salt.
2. In a separate bowl, cream together the butter and brown sugar until light and fluffy.
3. Beat in the egg and vanilla extract.
4. Gradually add the flour mixture to the butter mixture and mix until a dough forms.
5. Stir in the crushed digestive biscuits, marshmallows, and chocolate chips.
6. Divide the dough into 8-10 equal pieces and shape each piece into a ball.
7. Place the cookie dough balls into the air fryer basket, leaving some space in between each one.
8. Cook the cookies in the air fryer at 160°C for 10-12 minutes, or until they are golden brown.
9. Remove the cookies from the air fryer and let them cool on a wire rack before serving. Enjoy!

White Chocolate Macadamia Nut Cookies

INGREDIENTS

- 200g all-purpose flour
- 1/2 tsp baking powder
- 1/4 tsp baking soda
- 1/4 tsp salt
- 1 egg
- 115 g unsalted butter, room temperature
- 100g granulated sugar
- 75g brown sugar
- 1 tsp vanilla extract
- 100g white chocolate chips
- 60g macadamia nuts, chopped

 Cooking Time 10 Minutes **Servings** 24

INSTRUCTION

1. In a mixing bowl, whisk together the flour, baking powder, baking soda, and salt.
2. In a separate bowl, beat the butter with the granulated sugar and brown sugar until light and fluffy.
3. Mix in the egg and vanilla extract until well combined.
4. Add the dry ingredients to the wet mixture and stir until a dough forms.
5. Fold in the white chocolate chips and chopped macadamia nuts.
6. Cover the dough with plastic wrap and refrigerate for at least 30 minutes or overnight.
7. Preheat your air fryer to 175°C.
8. Roll the dough into 1 inch balls and place them on a greased air fryer basket, leaving space between them.
9. Flatten each ball slightly with the back of a fork.
10. Air fry the cookies for 8 to 10 minutes or until lightly golden brown.
11. Let the cookies cool on the basket for 5 minutes before transferring them to a wire rack to cool completely.

Almond Cookies

INGREDIENTS

- 200g all-purpose flour
- 100g almond flour
- 1/2 tsp baking powder
- 1/4 tsp salt
- 100g unsalted butter, softened
- 150g granulated sugar
- 1 large egg
- 1/2 tsp vanilla extract
- 50g sliced almonds

 Cooking Time 10 Minutes   **Servings** 20

INSTRUCTION

1. Preheat your air fryer to 180°C.
2. In a mixing bowl, whisk together the all-purpose flour, almond flour, baking powder, and salt.
3. In a separate mixing bowl, cream together the softened unsalted butter and granulated sugar until light and fluffy.
4. Beat in the egg and vanilla extract until well combined.
5. Add the dry ingredients to the wet ingredients and mix until just combined.
6. Roll the dough into small balls and place them on a lined air fryer basket, making sure to leave some space between each cookie.
7. Flatten each cookie slightly with the palm of your hand, and sprinkle some sliced almonds on top of each cookie, pressing them in slightly.
8. Air fry the cookies for 8-10 minutes, until they are lightly golden brown.
9. Remove the cookies from the air fryer and let them cool on a wire rack.

Peanut Butter Chocolate Chip Cookies

INGREDIENTS

- 195g all-purpose flour
- 115g unsalted butter, room temperature
- 120g smooth peanut butter
- 150g granulated sugar
- 1/2 tsp baking powder
- 1/4 tsp baking soda
- 1/4 tsp salt
- 1 egg
- 1 tsp vanilla extract
- 100g chocolate chips

 Cooking Time 10 Minutes   **Servings** 24

INSTRUCTION

1. In a mixing bowl, whisk together the flour, baking powder, baking soda, and salt.
2. In a separate bowl, beat the butter, peanut butter, and granulated sugar until light and fluffy.
3. Mix in the egg and vanilla extract until well combined.
4. Add the dry ingredients to the wet mixture and stir until a dough forms.
5. Fold in the chocolate chips.
6. Cover the dough with plastic wrap and refrigerate for at least 30 minutes or overnight.
7. Preheat your air fryer to 175°C.
8. Roll the dough into 1 inch balls and place them on a greased air fryer basket, leaving space between them.
9. Flatten each ball slightly with the back of a fork.
10. Air fry the cookies for 8 to 10 minutes or until lightly golden brown.
11. Let the cookies cool on the basket for 5 minutes before transferring them to a wire rack to cool completely.

Raspberry Thumbprint Cookies

INGREDIENTS

- 200g flour
- 1 egg yolk
- 1/2 tsp vanilla extract
- 100g unsalted butter, at room temperature
- 50g granulated sugar
- 50g raspberry jam or preserves

 Cooking Time
10 Minutes

 Servings
18

INSTRUCTION

1. In a mixing bowl, whisk together the flour and salt.
2. In a separate bowl, beat the butter and sugar until light and fluffy.
3. Mix in the egg yolk and vanilla extract until well combined.
4. Add the flour mixture to the wet mixture and stir until a dough forms.
5. Cover the dough with plastic wrap and refrigerate for at least 30 minutes or overnight.
6. Preheat your air fryer to 175°C.
7. Roll the dough into 1 inch balls and place them on a greased air fryer basket, leaving space between them.
8. Press your thumb into the center of each ball to make a small indentation.
9. Drop a small amount of raspberry jam or preserves into the center of each indentation.
10. Air fry the cookies for 8 to 10 minutes or until lightly golden brown.
11. Let the cookies cool on the basket for 5 minutes before transferring them to a wire rack to cool completely.

Chocolate Crinkle Cookies

INGREDIENTS

- 200g all-purpose flour
- 50g unsweetened cocoa powder
- 115g unsalted butter, room temperature
- 150g granulated sugar
- 1 tsp baking powder
- 1/4 tsp salt
- 2 eggs
- 1 tsp vanilla extract
- 100g powdered sugar

 Cooking Time
10 Minutes

 Servings
24

INSTRUCTION

1. In a mixing bowl, whisk together the flour, cocoa powder, baking powder, and salt.
2. In a separate bowl, beat the butter and granulated sugar until light and fluffy.
3. Mix in the eggs and vanilla extract until well combined.
4. Add the dry ingredients to the wet mixture and stir until a dough forms.
5. Cover the dough with plastic wrap and refrigerate for at least 30 minutes or overnight.
6. Preheat your air fryer to 175°C.
7. Roll the dough into 1 inch balls and coat them generously in powdered sugar.
8. Place the coated balls on a greased air fryer basket, leaving space between them.
9. Air fry the cookies for 8 to 10 minutes or until lightly golden brown.
10. Let the cookies cool on the basket for 5 minutes before transferring them to a wire rack to cool completely.

Chocolate Covered Pretzel Cookies

INGREDIENTS

- 175 g all-purpose flour
- 70 g unsweetened cocoa powder
- 1/2 tsp baking powder
- 150 g granulated sugar
- 1 egg
- 1/4 tsp salt
- 115 g unsalted butter, room temperature
- 1 tsp vanilla extract
- 100 g small pretzels, crushed
- 100 g chocolate chips or chopped chocolate

 Cooking Time 10 Minutes   **Servings** 24

INSTRUCTION

1. In a mixing bowl, whisk together the flour, cocoa powder, baking powder, and salt.
2. In a separate bowl, beat the butter and granulated sugar until light and fluffy.
3. Mix in the egg and vanilla extract until well combined.
4. Add the dry ingredients to the wet mixture and stir until a dough forms.
5. Fold in the crushed pretzels and chocolate chips or chopped chocolate.
6. Cover the dough with plastic wrap and refrigerate for at least 30 minutes or overnight.
7. Preheat your air fryer to 175°C.
8. Roll the dough into 1 inch balls and place them on a greased air fryer basket, leaving space between them.
9. Flatten each ball slightly with the palm of your hand.
10. Air fry the cookies for 8 to 10 minutes or until lightly golden brown.
11. Let the cookies cool on the basket for 5 minutes before transferring them to a wire rack to cool completely.

Butter Cookies

INGREDIENTS

- 200g all-purpose flour
- 1 egg yolk
- 1/2 tsp vanilla extract
- 115 g unsalted butter, room temperature
- 50g granulated sugar

 Cooking Time
10 Minutes

 Servings
18-20

INSTRUCTION

1. In a mixing bowl, whisk together the flour and salt.
2. In a separate bowl, beat the butter and granulated sugar until light and fluffy.
3. Mix in the egg yolk and vanilla extract until well combined.
4. Add the flour mixture to the wet mixture and stir until a dough forms.
5. Cover the dough with plastic wrap and refrigerate for at least 30 minutes or overnight.
6. Preheat your air fryer to 175°C.
7. Roll the dough out to a thickness of 1/4 inch and cut out shapes with a cookie cutter.
8. Place the cookies on a greased air fryer basket, leaving space between them.
9. Air fry the cookies for 8 to 10 minutes or until lightly golden brown.
10. Let the cookies cool on the basket for 5 minutes before transferring them to a wire rack to cool completely.

Cinnamon Sugar Cookies

INGREDIENTS

- 200g all-purpose flour
- 1 tsp baking powder
- 100g granulated sugar
- 1 egg
- 1/2 tsp ground cinnamon
- 1/4 tsp salt
- 115g unsalted butter, room temperature
- 1 tsp vanilla extract
- 50g granulated sugar (for coating)
- 1 tsp ground cinnamon (for coating)

 Cooking Time 10 Minutes   Servings 24

INSTRUCTION

1. In a mixing bowl, whisk together the flour, baking powder, cinnamon, and salt.
2. In a separate bowl, beat the butter and granulated sugar until light and fluffy.
3. Mix in the egg and vanilla extract until well combined.
4. Add the dry ingredients to the wet mixture and stir until a dough forms.
5. Cover the dough with plastic wrap and refrigerate for at least 30 minutes or overnight.
6. Preheat your air fryer to 175°C.
7. In a small bowl, mix together the 50 g granulated sugar and 1 tsp ground cinnamon.
8. Roll the dough into 1 inch balls and coat them generously in the cinnamon sugar mixture.
9. Place the coated balls on a greased air fryer basket, leaving space between them.
10. Air fry the cookies for 8 to 10 minutes or until lightly golden brown.
11. Let the cookies cool on the basket for 5 minutes before transferring them to a wire rack to cool completely.

Strawberry Muffins

INGREDIENTS

- 200g all-purpose flour
- 1 1/2 tsp baking powder
- 1/4 tsp salt
- 100g caster sugar
- 2 medium eggs
- 80ml vegetable oil
- 80ml milk
- 150g fresh strawberries, chopped

 Cooking Time 15 Minutes   **Servings** 6

INSTRUCTION

1. In a mixing bowl, combine the flour, baking powder, and salt.
2. In a separate bowl, whisk together the caster sugar, eggs, vegetable oil, and milk until well combined.
3. Pour the wet mixture into the dry mixture, and mix until just combined.
4. Fold in the chopped strawberries.
5. Spoon the muffin mixture into 6 silicone muffin cups, filling each about 2/3 full.
6. Cook the muffins in the air fryer at 180°C for 12-15 minutes, or until a toothpick comes out clean.
7. Let the muffins cool for 5 minutes before serving

Cranberry Orange Muffins

INGREDIENTS

- 200g all-purpose flour
- 1 1/2 tsp baking powder
- 1/4 tsp baking soda
- 1/4 tsp salt
- 100g caster sugar
- 2 medium eggs
- 80ml vegetable oil
- 80ml milk
- 1 medium orange, zested and juiced
- 100g fresh or frozen cranberries, roughly chopped

 Cooking Time
15 Minutes

 Servings
6

INSTRUCTION

1. In a mixing bowl, combine the flour, baking powder, baking soda, salt, and caster sugar.
2. In a separate bowl, whisk together the eggs, vegetable oil, milk, orange zest, and orange juice until well combined.
3. Pour the wet mixture into the dry mixture, and mix until just combined.
4. Fold in the chopped cranberries.
5. Spoon the muffin mixture into 6 silicone muffin cups, filling each about 2/3 full.
6. Cook the muffins in the air fryer at 180°C for 12-15 minutes, or until a toothpick comes out clean.
7. Let the muffins cool for 5 minutes before serving.

Carrot Muffins

INGREDIENTS

- 200g all-purpose flour
- 1 1/2 tsp baking powder
- 1/2 tsp baking soda
- 1/4 tsp salt
- 100g caster sugar
- 2 medium eggs
- 80ml vegetable oil
- 80ml milk
- 1 medium carrot, grated
- 50g chopped walnuts (optional)

 Cooking Time
15 Minutes

 Servings
6

INSTRUCTION

1. In a mixing bowl, combine the flour, baking powder, baking soda, salt, and caster sugar.
2. In a separate bowl, whisk together the eggs, vegetable oil, and milk until well combined.
3. Pour the wet mixture into the dry mixture, and mix until just combined.
4. Fold in the grated carrot and chopped walnuts (if using).
5. Spoon the muffin mixture into 6 silicone muffin cups, filling each about 2/3 full.
6. Cook the muffins in the air fryer at 180°C for 12-15 minutes, or until a toothpick comes out clean.
7. Let the muffins cool for 5 minutes before serving

Chocolate Zucchini Muffins

INGREDIENTS

- 150g all-purpose flour
- 30g cocoa powder
- 1 tsp baking powder
- 1/2 tsp baking soda
- 1/4 tsp salt
- 80g caster sugar
- 1 medium egg
- 60ml vegetable oil
- 80ml milk
- 100g zucchini, grated
- 50g chocolate chips

 Cooking Time
15 Minutes   **Servings**
6

INSTRUCTION

1. In a mixing bowl, combine the flour, cocoa powder, baking powder, baking soda, salt, and caster sugar.
2. In a separate bowl, whisk together the egg, vegetable oil, and milk until well combined.
3. Pour the wet mixture into the dry mixture, and mix until just combined.
4. Fold in the grated zucchini and chocolate chips.
5. Spoon the muffin mixture into 6 silicone muffin cups, filling each about 2/3 full.
6. Cook the muffins in the air fryer at 180°C for 12-15 minutes, or until a toothpick comes out clean.
7. Let the muffins cool for 5 minutes before serving.

Blueberry Banana Muffins

INGREDIENTS

- 200g all-purpose flour
- 1 1/2 tsp baking powder
- 1/2 tsp baking soda
- 1/4 tsp salt
- 100g caster sugar
- 2 medium ripe bananas, mashed
- 2 medium eggs
- 80ml vegetable oil
- 80ml milk
- 100g fresh or frozen blueberries

 Cooking Time
15 Minutes

 Servings
6

INSTRUCTION

1. In a mixing bowl, combine the flour, baking powder, baking soda, salt, and caster sugar.
2. In a separate bowl, whisk together the mashed bananas, eggs, vegetable oil, and milk until well combined.
3. Pour the wet mixture into the dry mixture, and mix until just combined.
4. Fold in the blueberries.
5. Spoon the muffin mixture into 6 silicone muffin cups, filling each about 2/3 full.
6. Cook the muffins in the air fryer at 180°C for 12-15 minutes, or until a toothpick comes out clean.
7. Let the muffins cool for 5 minutes before serving

Chocolate Cherry Muffins

INGREDIENTS

- 150g all-purpose flour
- 30g cocoa powder
- 1 tsp baking powder
- 1/2 tsp baking soda
- 1/4 tsp salt
- 80g caster sugar
- 1 medium egg
- 60ml vegetable oil
- 80ml milk
- 50g chocolate chips
- 100g pitted cherries, chopped.

Cooking Time
15 Minutes

Servings
6

INSTRUCTION

1. In a mixing bowl, combine the flour, cocoa powder, baking powder, baking soda, salt, and caster sugar.
2. In a separate bowl, whisk together the egg, vegetable oil, and milk until well combined.
3. Pour the wet mixture into the dry mixture, and mix until just combined.
4. Fold in the chocolate chips and chopped cherries.
5. Spoon the muffin mixture into 6 silicone muffin cups, filling each about 2/3 full.
6. Cook the muffins in the air fryer at 180°C for 12-15 minutes, or until a toothpick comes out clean.
7. Let the muffins cool for 5 minutes before serving.

Lemon Blueberry Muffins

INGREDIENTS

- 200g all-purpose flour
- 1 1/2 tsp baking powder
- 1/2 tsp baking soda
- 1/4 tsp salt
- 100g caster sugar
- 2 medium eggs
- 80ml vegetable oil
- 80ml milk
- 1 lemon, zest and juice
- 100g fresh or frozen blueberries

 Cooking Time
15 Minutes   **Servings**
6

INSTRUCTION

1. In a mixing bowl, combine the flour, baking powder, baking soda, salt, and caster sugar.
2. In a separate bowl, whisk together the eggs, vegetable oil, milk, lemon zest, and lemon juice until well combined.
3. Pour the wet mixture into the dry mixture, and mix until just combined.
4. Fold in the blueberries.
5. Spoon the muffin mixture into 6 silicone muffin cups, filling each about 2/3 full.
6. Cook the muffins in the air fryer at 180°C for 12-15 minutes, or until a toothpick comes out clean.
7. Let the muffins cool for 5 minutes before serving.

Mixed Berry Muffins

INGREDIENTS

- 200g all-purpose flour
- 1 1/2 tsp baking powder
- 1/2 tsp baking soda
- 1/4 tsp salt
- 100g caster sugar
- 2 medium eggs
- 80ml vegetable oil
- 80ml milk
- 100g mixed berries (e.g. raspberries, blackberries, and blueberries)

 Cooking Time
15 Minutes

 Servings
6

INSTRUCTION

1. In a mixing bowl, combine the flour, baking powder, baking soda, salt, and caster sugar.
2. In a separate bowl, whisk together the eggs, vegetable oil, and milk until well combined.
3. Pour the wet mixture into the dry mixture, and mix until just combined.
4. Fold in the mixed berries.
5. Spoon the muffin mixture into 6 silicone muffin cups, filling each about 2/3 full.
6. Cook the muffins in the air fryer at 180°C for 12-15 minutes, or until a toothpick comes out clean.
7. Let the muffins cool for 5 minutes before serving.

Banana Nut Muffins

INGREDIENTS

- 200g all-purpose flour
- 1 1/2 tsp baking powder
- 1/2 tsp baking soda
- 1/4 tsp salt
- 100g caster sugar
- 2 medium ripe bananas, mashed
- 2 medium eggs
- 80ml vegetable oil
- 80ml milk
- 50g chopped walnuts

 Cooking Time
15 Minutes

 Servings
6

INSTRUCTION

1. In a mixing bowl, combine the flour, baking powder, baking soda, salt, and caster sugar.
2. In a separate bowl, whisk together the mashed bananas, eggs, vegetable oil, and milk until well combined.
3. Pour the wet mixture into the dry mixture, and mix until just combined.
4. Fold in the chopped walnuts.
5. Spoon the muffin mixture into 6 silicone muffin cups, filling each about 2/3 full.
6. Cook the muffins in the air fryer at 180°C for 12-15 minutes, or until a toothpick comes out clean.
7. Let the muffins cool for 5 minutes before serving.

Pumpkin Muffins

INGREDIENTS

- 200g all-purpose flour
- 1 1/2 tsp baking powder
- 1/2 tsp baking soda
- 1/4 tsp salt
- 100g caster sugar
- 1 tsp ground cinnamon
- 1/2 tsp ground ginger
- 1/4 tsp ground nutmeg
- 1/4 tsp ground cloves
- 120g pumpkin puree
- 2 medium eggs
- 80ml vegetable oil
- 80ml milk

INSTRUCTION

1. In a mixing bowl, combine the flour, baking powder, baking soda, salt, caster sugar, cinnamon, ginger, nutmeg, and cloves.
2. In a separate bowl, whisk together the pumpkin puree, eggs, vegetable oil, and milk until well combined.
3. Pour the wet mixture into the dry mixture, and mix until just combined.
4. Spoon the muffin mixture into 6 silicone muffin cups, filling each about 2/3 full.
5. Cook the muffins in the air fryer at 180°C for 12-15 minutes, or until a toothpick comes out clean.
6. Let the muffins cool for 5 minutes before serving.

Blueberry Muffins

INGREDIENTS

- 120g all-purpose flour
- 1 tsp baking powder
- 1/4 tsp baking soda
- 1/4 tsp salt
- 50g caster sugar
- 1 large egg
- 60ml milk
- 2 tbsp vegetable oil
- 1/2 tsp vanilla extract
- 100g fresh blueberries

 Cooking Time
12 Minutes

 Servings
6

INSTRUCTION

1. In a mixing bowl, whisk together the all-purpose flour, baking powder, baking soda, salt, and caster sugar.
2. In another mixing bowl, whisk together the egg, milk, vegetable oil, and vanilla extract.
3. Gradually add the wet ingredients to the dry ingredients, stirring until just combined.
4. Gently fold in the fresh blueberries.
5. Spoon the muffin batter into greased muffin cups or silicone liners, filling them about 2/3 of the way full.
6. Preheat the air fryer at 160°C for 3-5 minutes.
7. Place the muffin cups or liners in the air fryer basket, and cook for 10-12 minutes, or until a toothpick inserted into the centre of a muffin comes out clean.
8. Let the muffins cool for a few minutes before removing them from the muffin cups or liners. Serve warm or at room temperature.

Lemon Poppy Seed Muffins

INGREDIENTS

- 120g all-purpose flour
- 1 tsp baking powder
- 1/4 tsp baking soda
- 1/4 tsp salt
- 50g caster sugar
- 1 large egg
- 60ml milk
- 2 tbsp vegetable oil
- 1/2 tsp vanilla extract
- 1 tbsp poppy seeds
- Zest of 1 lemon
- Juice of 1/2 lemon.

 Cooking Time 12 Minutes   **Servings** 6

INSTRUCTION

1. In a mixing bowl, whisk together the all-purpose flour, baking powder, baking soda, salt, and caster sugar.
2. In another mixing bowl, whisk together the egg, milk, vegetable oil, vanilla extract, poppy seeds, lemon zest, and lemon juice.
3. Gradually add the wet ingredients to the dry ingredients, stirring until just combined.
4. Spoon the muffin batter into greased muffin cups or silicone liners, filling them about 2/3 of the way full.
5. Preheat the air fryer at 160°C for 3-5 minutes.
6. Place the muffin cups or liners in the air fryer basket, and cook for 10-12 minutes, or until a toothpick inserted into the centre of a muffin comes out clean.
7. Let the muffins cool for a few minutes before removing them from the muffin cups or liners. Serve warm or at room temperature.

Chocolate Chip Muffins

INGREDIENTS

- 200g all-purpose flour
- 2 tsp baking powder
- 1/4 tsp salt
- 50g caster sugar
- 100g chocolate chips
- 1 large egg
- 180ml milk
- 2 tbsp vegetable oil
- 1 tsp vanilla extract

 Cooking Time
15 Minutes

 Servings
6

INSTRUCTION

1. In a mixing bowl, whisk together the all-purpose flour, baking powder, salt, caster sugar, and chocolate chips.
2. In another mixing bowl, whisk together the egg, milk, vegetable oil, and vanilla extract.
3. Gradually add the wet ingredients to the dry ingredients, stirring until just combined.
4. Spoon the muffin batter into greased muffin cups or silicone liners, filling them about 2/3 of the way full.
5. Preheat the air fryer at 160°C for 3-5 minutes.
6. Place the muffin cups or liners in the air fryer basket, and cook for 12-15 minutes, or until a toothpick inserted into the centre of a muffin comes out clean.
7. Let the muffins cool for a few minutes before removing them from the muffin cups or liners. Serve warm or at room temperature.

Brownies

INGREDIENTS

- 125g unsalted butter
- 200g caster sugar
- 2 large eggs
- 60g all-purpose flour
- 50g unsweetened cocoa powder
- 1/2 tsp baking powder
- 1/4 tsp salt

 Cooking Time 18 Minutes   **Servings** 6-8

INSTRUCTION

1. Melt the butter in a saucepan over low heat. Once melted, remove from heat and stir in the caster sugar until well combined.
2. Beat in the eggs, one at a time, until well incorporated.
3. In a separate bowl, whisk together the all-purpose flour, cocoa powder, baking powder, and salt.
4. Gradually add the dry ingredients to the wet ingredients, stirring until just combined.
5. Spoon the brownie batter into a greased 6-inch square baking pan.
6. Preheat the air fryer at 160°C for 3-5 minutes.
7. Place the baking pan in the air fryer basket and cook for 15-18 minutes or until a toothpick inserted into the centre of the brownies comes out with a few moist crumbs attached.
8. Allow the brownies to cool in the pan for 10-15 minutes before slicing and serving. Enjoy!

Lemon Bars

INGREDIENTS

for the Crust:
- 125g unsalted butter, softened
- 50g caster sugar
- 175g plain flour
- pinch of salt

for the Filling:
- 4 medium eggs
- 200g caster sugar
- 3 tbsp plain flour
- zest of 2 lemons
- 125ml fresh lemon juice
- icing sugar, for dusting

INSTRUCTION

 Cooking Time 30 Minutes   **Servings** 9-12

1. In a large mixing bowl, beat the softened butter and sugar together until creamy and pale.
2. Sift in the plain flour and salt, and mix with a wooden spoon until a crumbly dough forms.
3. Lightly grease an 8-inch square baking tin with butter, or line with parchment paper.
4. Press the dough into the bottom of the tin, smoothing it out with your fingers to form an even layer.
5. Place the tin into the air fryer basket and bake at 160°C for 10 minutes.
6. In the meantime, prepare the filling. In a mixing bowl, whisk the eggs and caster sugar together until pale and frothy.
7. Sift the plain flour over the mixture and whisk again until smooth.
8. Add the lemon zest and lemon juice, and whisk until well combined.
9. Pour the filling mixture over the partially-baked crust in the tin.
10. Place the tin back into the air fryer basket and bake at 160°C for 20-25 minutes until the filling is set and slightly firm to the touch.
11. Remove the Lemon Bars from the basket and let them cool completely in the tin before cutting.
12. Dust the top with icing sugar, slice into squares and serve.

Blondies

INGREDIENTS

- 200g unsalted butter, melted
- 300g light brown sugar
- 2 large eggs
- 1 tsp vanilla extract
- 250g plain flour
- 1/2 tsp baking powder
- 1/2 tsp salt
- 150g white chocolate chips.

 Cooking Time
20 Minutes

 Servings
12

INSTRUCTION

1. In a large bowl, mix together the melted butter and light brown sugar until well combined.
2. Add the eggs and vanilla extract, and mix well.
3. In a separate bowl, whisk together the flour, baking powder, and salt.
4. Add the dry ingredients to the wet ingredients, and mix until just combined.
5. Fold in the white chocolate chips.
6. Grease the air fryer basket with cooking spray or butter.
7. Pour the blondie batter into the basket and spread evenly.
8. Place the basket in the air fryer and cook at 180°C for 15-20 minutes or until a toothpick inserted in the center comes out clean.
9. Let the blondies cool in the basket for a few minutes before transferring them to a wire rack to cool completely.
10. Cut into squares and serve.

Raspberry Bars

INGREDIENTS

- 200g plain flour
- 75g caster sugar
- 1/4 tsp salt
- 150g unsalted butter, softened
- 150g raspberry jam.

 Cooking Time
20 Minutes

 Servings
12

INSTRUCTION

1. Preheat your air fryer to 160°C.
2. In a medium-sized mixing bowl, whisk together the flour, sugar, and salt.
3. Add the softened butter to the bowl and mix until the mixture becomes crumbly.
4. Reserve one cup of the crumb mixture and press the remaining mixture into the bottom of a greased 8-inch square baking dish.
5. Spread the raspberry jam over the crust.
6. Sprinkle the reserved crumb mixture over the top of the jam.
7. Place the baking dish in the air fryer basket and cook for 18-20 minutes, or until the edges of the bars are lightly golden.
8. Remove the dish from the air fryer and allow the bars to cool completely in the dish before slicing and serving.

Blondie Bars with Nuts

INGREDIENTS

- 150g unsalted butter, melted
- 220g light brown sugar
- 2 large eggs
- 2 tsp vanilla extract
- 180g plain flour
- 1/2 tsp baking powder
- 1/2 tsp salt
- 100g chopped nuts (such as pecans or walnuts)

 Cooking Time 25 Minutes   **Servings** 9

INSTRUCTION

1. In a mixing bowl, whisk together the melted butter and brown sugar until well combined.
2. Add the eggs and vanilla extract, and whisk again until smooth.
3. In a separate bowl, sift together the flour, baking powder, and salt.
4. Gradually stir the dry ingredients into the wet ingredients, mixing until just combined.
5. Fold in the chopped nuts.
6. Grease a square baking dish that fits inside your air fryer basket with cooking spray, and pour the blondie batter into the dish.
7. Preheat your air fryer to 160°C.
8. Once preheated, place the baking dish into the air fryer basket and cook for 20-25 minutes or until the edges are golden brown and the center is set.
9. Let the blondies cool in the dish for 5 minutes before slicing and serving.

Brown Sugar Bars

INGREDIENTS

- 200g plain flour
- 150g light brown sugar
- 120g unsalted butter, softened
- 1 egg
- 1 tsp vanilla extract
- 1/2 tsp baking powder
- 1/4 tsp salt

 Cooking Time 18 Minutes   **Servings** 12

INSTRUCTION

1. Preheat your air fryer to 180°C.
2. In a medium bowl, cream together the butter and brown sugar until light and fluffy.
3. Add the egg and vanilla extract, and mix until well combined.
4. In a separate bowl, whisk together the flour, baking powder, and salt.
5. Add the dry ingredients to the wet ingredients, and mix until just combined.
6. Press the mixture into the bottom of an 8-inch square baking dish that will fit in your air fryer basket.
7. Place the baking dish in the air fryer basket and cook for 15-18 minutes, or until the bars are golden brown and a toothpick inserted into the center comes out clean.
8. Allow the bars to cool completely before cutting into squares and serving

Reese's Bars

INGREDIENTS

- 175g milk chocolate chips
- 60g unsalted butter
- 175g creamy peanut butter
- 70g icing sugar
- 120g digestive biscuits, crushed
- 1/2 teaspoon vanilla extract
- Pinch of salt

 Cooking Time 12 Minutes   **Servings** 16

INSTRUCTION

1. Preheat your air fryer to 180°C.
2. In a microwave-safe bowl, combine the milk chocolate chips and unsalted butter. Melt in the microwave in 30-second intervals, stirring in between, until smooth.
3. In a separate bowl, mix together the peanut butter, icing sugar, crushed digestive biscuits, vanilla extract, and salt until well combined.
4. Grease an 8x8 inch baking dish with cooking spray and press half of the peanut butter mixture into the bottom of the dish.
5. Pour the melted chocolate over the peanut butter mixture and spread evenly.
6. Drop spoonfuls of the remaining peanut butter mixture on top of the chocolate, using a knife or spatula to swirl the two layers together.
7. Place the baking dish in the air fryer basket and cook for 10-12 minutes, or until the top is set and the edges are slightly browned.
8. Let cool completely before cutting into bars and serving. Enjoy!

Cinnamon Sugar Donuts

INGREDIENTS

- 125g all-purpose flour
- 2 tsp baking powder
- 1/4 tsp salt
- 50g granulated sugar
- 1 egg
- 60ml whole milk
- 2 tbsp unsalted butter, melted
- 1 tsp vanilla extract
- 50g granulated sugar
- 1 tsp ground cinnamon
- 2 tbsp unsalted butter, melted

 Cooking Time
6 Minutes   **Servings**
6

INSTRUCTION

1. In a medium bowl, whisk together the flour, baking powder, salt, and sugar.
2. In a separate bowl, whisk together the egg, milk, melted butter, and vanilla extract.
3. Add the wet ingredients to the dry ingredients and stir until just combined.
4. Lightly grease the air fryer basket with cooking spray.
5. Spoon the batter into a piping bag or a zip-top bag with a corner snipped off. Pipe the batter into the air fryer basket, filling each well about 2/3 of the way full.
6. Air fry at 180°C for 4-6 minutes, until the donuts are golden brown and cooked through.
7. In a shallow bowl, whisk together the sugar and cinnamon.
8. As soon as the donuts are cool enough to handle, brush each one with melted butter and roll in the cinnamon sugar mixture until coated.
9. Serve warm and enjoy!

Lemon Donuts

INGREDIENTS

- 150g all-purpose flour
- 50g granulated sugar
- 1/2 tsp baking powder
- 1/4 tsp baking soda
- 1/4 tsp salt
- 1 egg
- 60ml buttermilk
- 1 tbsp unsalted butter, melted
- 2 tbsp freshly squeezed lemon juice
- 1 tbsp lemon zest
- Icing sugar, for dusting

 Cooking Time 8 Minutes   Servings 6-8

INSTRUCTION

1. In a mixing bowl, whisk together the flour, sugar, baking powder, baking soda, and salt until combined.
2. In a separate bowl, whisk together the egg, buttermilk, melted butter, lemon juice, and lemon zest until well combined.
3. Pour the wet ingredients into the dry ingredients and stir until just combined. The batter should be thick and slightly lumpy.
4. Spoon the batter into a piping bag or a large plastic bag with one corner cut off.
5. Pipe the batter into the donut molds of your air fryer, filling them about two-thirds full.
6. Cook the donuts in the air fryer at 180°C for 6-8 minutes or until golden brown and a toothpick inserted into the center comes out clean.
7. Remove the donuts from the air fryer and let them cool for a few minutes.
8. Dust the donuts with icing sugar and serve.

Chocolate Donuts

INGREDIENTS

- 100g all-purpose flour
- 25g unsweetened cocoa powder
- 1 tsp baking powder
- 1/4 tsp baking soda
- 1/4 tsp salt
- 50g granulated sugar
- 60ml milk
- 1 large egg
- 2 tbsp vegetable oil
- 1 tsp vanilla extract
- 100g chocolate chips

INSTRUCTION

 Cooking Time 10 Minutes **Servings** 6-8

1. In a bowl, whisk together flour, cocoa powder, baking powder, baking soda, salt, and sugar.
2. In a separate bowl, whisk together milk, egg, vegetable oil, and vanilla extract until smooth.
3. Gradually add the wet ingredients to the dry ingredients and stir until just combined. Fold in the chocolate chips.
4. Grease the air fryer basket with cooking spray or oil. Fill each donut mold about 2/3 full with batter.
5. Cook in the air fryer at 180°C for 8-10 minutes or until a toothpick inserted into the center of a donut comes out clean.
6. Remove the donuts from the air fryer and allow to cool in the mold for a few minutes before removing and transferring to a wire rack to cool completely.
7. Repeat with any remaining batter.

Vanilla Donuts

INGREDIENTS

- 150g all-purpose flour
- 70g granulated sugar
- 1 tsp baking powder
- 1/4 tsp salt
- 1 large egg
- 120ml milk
- 2 tbsp unsalted butter, melted
- 1 tsp vanilla extract

 Cooking Time
10 Minutes

 Servings
6-8

INSTRUCTION

1. In a medium bowl, whisk together the flour, sugar, baking powder, and salt.
2. In a separate bowl, beat the egg and then whisk in the milk, melted butter, and vanilla extract.
3. Add the wet ingredients to the dry ingredients and stir until just combined. Do not overmix.
4. Spoon the batter into a greased donut pan, filling each mold about 3/4 full.
5. Place the pan into the air fryer basket and set the temperature to 180°C. Bake for 8-10 minutes or until a toothpick inserted into the center of a donut comes out clean.
6. Let the donuts cool in the pan for a few minutes before removing them and placing them on a wire rack to cool completely.
7. Repeat with any remaining batter.
8. Once cooled, you can decorate the donuts with glaze, sprinkles, or any other toppings of your choice. Enjoy!

Strawberry Donuts

INGREDIENTS

- 100g all-purpose flour
- 50g granulated sugar
- 1 tsp baking powder
- 1/4 tsp salt
- 1 egg
- 60ml whole milk
- 20g unsalted butter, melted
- 1/2 tsp vanilla extract
- 50g fresh strawberries, finely chopped
- Powdered sugar, for dusting

 Cooking Time 8 Minutes   **Servings** 6

INSTRUCTION

1. In a mixing bowl, whisk together the flour, sugar, baking powder, and salt.
2. In another bowl, beat the egg and then mix in the milk, melted butter, and vanilla extract.
3. Add the wet ingredients to the dry ingredients and mix until just combined.
4. Fold in the chopped strawberries.
5. Spray the air fryer basket with cooking spray.
6. Spoon the batter into a piping bag and pipe the batter into the air fryer basket, filling each mold halfway.
7. Air fry at 180°C for 7-8 minutes, or until the donuts are golden brown and a toothpick inserted in the center comes out clean.
8. Let the donuts cool in the air fryer for a few minutes before removing them from the basket.
9. Dust the donuts with powdered sugar before serving.

Glazed Donuts

INGREDIENTS

- 250g plain flour
- 50g caster sugar
- 1 tbsp baking powder
- 1/4 tsp salt
- 120ml milk
- 1 egg
- 1 tsp vanilla extract
- 2 tbsp melted butter

For the glaze:
- 100g icing sugar
- 2 tbsp milk
- 1/2 tsp vanilla extract

INSTRUCTION

 Cooking Time 10 Minutes **Servings** 8-10

1. In a large mixing bowl, whisk together the flour, caster sugar, baking powder, and salt.
2. In a separate bowl, whisk together the milk, egg, vanilla extract, and melted butter.
3. Pour the wet ingredients into the dry ingredients and mix until just combined.
4. Place the mixture into a piping bag or ziplock bag and pipe the batter into the donut molds of the air fryer.
5. Set the air fryer to 160°C and cook the donuts for 8-10 minutes until they are golden brown.
6. While the donuts are cooking, prepare the glaze by whisking together the icing sugar, milk, and vanilla extract until smooth.
7. Once the donuts are done, remove them from the air fryer and let them cool for a few minutes.
8. Dip each donut into the glaze, then set them aside to allow the glaze to set.

S'mores Donuts

INGREDIENTS

- 100g all-purpose flour
- 50g granulated sugar
- 1 tsp baking powder
- 1/4 tsp salt
- 60ml milk
- 1 egg
- 1 tbsp vegetable oil
- 1/2 tsp vanilla extract
- 3 tbsp graham cracker crumbs
- 3 tbsp mini chocolate chips
- 3 tbsp mini marshmallows

For the Glaze:
- 50g powdered sugar
- 1 tbsp milk
- 1 tbsp graham cracker crumbs
- 1 tbsp mini chocolate chips
- 1 tbsp mini marshmallows

INSTRUCTION

1. In a mixing bowl, whisk together the flour, sugar, baking powder, and salt.
2. In a separate bowl, mix together the milk, egg, vegetable oil, and vanilla extract.
3. Add the wet ingredients to the dry ingredients and mix until well combined.
4. Fold in the graham cracker crumbs, mini chocolate chips, and mini marshmallows.
5. Grease the air fryer basket with cooking spray and pour the batter into a piping bag.
6. Pipe the batter into the donut molds and make sure to leave some space for the donuts to expand.
7. Cook the donuts in the air fryer at 180°C for 6-8 minutes or until they are golden brown.
8. Remove the donuts from the air fryer and allow them to cool.
9. In a mixing bowl, whisk together the powdered sugar and milk until smooth.
10. Dip the cooled donuts into the glaze and sprinkle with graham cracker crumbs, mini chocolate chips, and mini marshmallows.

 Cooking Time 8 Minutes

 Servings 6

Maple Donuts

INGREDIENTS

- 250g all-purpose flour
- 100g granulated sugar
- 2 tsp baking powder
- 1/2 tsp salt
- 1/4 tsp ground nutmeg
- 1/4 tsp ground cinnamon
- 1 egg
- 120ml milk
- 60g unsalted butter, melted
- 2 tbsp pure maple syrup

For the Glaze:

- 150g powdered sugar
- 3 tbsp pure maple syrup
- 2-3 tbsp milk

 Cooking Time 8 Minutes   **Servings** 12

INSTRUCTION

1. In a mixing bowl, combine the flour, sugar, baking powder, salt, nutmeg, and cinnamon.
2. In a separate bowl, beat the egg and then stir in the milk, melted butter, and maple syrup.
3. Add the wet ingredients to the dry ingredients and mix until just combined. Be careful not to overmix.
4. Spoon the batter into a piping bag and pipe the batter into a greased donut pan.
5. Air fry the donuts at 180°C for 6-8 minutes, or until they are golden brown and spring back when lightly touched.
6. Remove the donuts from the air fryer and let them cool for a few minutes before removing them from the pan and placing them on a wire rack to cool completely.
7. For the Glaze:
8. In a small bowl, whisk together the powdered sugar, maple syrup, and milk until the glaze is smooth and of a pourable consistency.
9. Dip each cooled donut into the glaze, allowing any excess glaze to drip off.
10. Let the glazed donuts sit for a few minutes to allow the glaze to set before serving.

Apple Cider Donuts

INGREDIENTS

- 280g all-purpose flour
- 10g baking powder
- 5g cinnamon
- 2g nutmeg
- 2g salt
- 115g unsalted butter, room temperature
- 150g granulated sugar
- 2 large eggs
- 120ml apple cider
- 1 tsp vanilla extract

For coating:
- 115g granulated sugar
- 2 tsp ground cinnamon
- 50g unsalted butter, melted

INSTRUCTION

1. In a medium bowl, whisk together the flour, baking powder, cinnamon, nutmeg, and salt.
2. In a large bowl, cream together the butter and sugar until light and fluffy. Add the eggs, one at a time, beating well after each addition. Stir in the apple cider and vanilla extract.
3. Gradually add the dry ingredients to the wet mixture, stirring until just combined.
4. Spoon the batter into a piping bag fitted with a large round tip. Pipe the batter into the air fryer donut molds, filling them about 2/3 of the way full.
5. Air fry the donuts at 180°C for 8-10 minutes, or until they are golden brown and cooked through.
6. In a small bowl, whisk together the granulated sugar and cinnamon for the coating.
7. Brush the melted butter over the warm donuts and then roll them in the cinnamon sugar mixture until fully coated.
8. Serve and enjoy your delicious Apple Cider Donuts!

 Cooking Time
10 Minutes

 Servings
12

Nutella Donuts

INGREDIENTS

- 120g all-purpose flour
- 1 tsp baking powder
- 1/4 tsp baking soda
- 1/4 tsp salt
- 50g granulated sugar
- 1 medium egg
- 80ml whole milk
- 1 tsp vanilla extract
- 2 tbsp vegetable oil
- 8 tsp Nutella
- Icing sugar, for dusting

 Cooking Time
8 Minutes

 Servings
8

INSTRUCTION

1. In a mixing bowl, combine the all-purpose flour, baking powder, baking soda, salt, and granulated sugar, and mix well.
2. Add the medium egg, whole milk, vanilla extract, and vegetable oil, and whisk until the batter is smooth and well combined.
3. Spoon the batter into a piping bag, and cut off the tip to create a small opening.
4. Grease the air fryer basket with a little vegetable oil.
5. Pipe the batter into the air fryer basket to create 8 evenly sized donuts, leaving enough space between each donut.
6. Spoon 1 tsp of Nutella onto the top of each donut, and use a toothpick to swirl it into the batter.
7. Close the air fryer basket and bake at 180°C for 6-8 minutes until the donuts are golden brown.
8. Remove the donuts from the air fryer basket and place them on a wire rack to cool slightly.
9. Dust the Nutella Donuts with icing sugar before serving. Enjoy!

Oreo Donuts

INGREDIENTS

- 150g plain flour
- 50g caster sugar
- 1 tsp baking powder
- 1/2 tsp salt
- 120ml milk
- 1 egg
- 1 tsp vanilla extract
- 50g melted butter
- 6 Oreo cookies, crushed
- 100g icing sugar
- 2 tbsp milk
- 6 Oreo cookies, crushed (for topping)

 Cooking Time 10 Minutes   Servings 6

INSTRUCTION

1. In a bowl, whisk together the flour, caster sugar, baking powder, and salt.
2. In a separate bowl, whisk together the milk, egg, and vanilla extract.
3. Gradually add the wet ingredients into the dry ingredients and stir until combined.
4. Stir in the melted butter and crushed Oreos until the batter is smooth.
5. Spoon the batter into a piping bag and pipe into a greased air fryer donut pan.
6. Cook in the air fryer at 180°C for 8-10 minutes or until the donuts are golden brown.
7. Allow the donuts to cool in the pan for a few minutes before removing them and placing them on a wire rack to cool completely.
8. While the donuts are cooling, make the glaze by whisking together the icing sugar and milk until smooth.
9. Dip each donut into the glaze and sprinkle with crushed Oreos on top.
10. Serve and enjoy!

Chocolate Chip Donuts

INGREDIENTS

- 120g all-purpose flour
- 40g granulated sugar
- 1 tsp baking powder
- 1/4 tsp salt
- 120ml milk
- 1 egg
- 2 tbsp unsalted butter, melted
- 1/2 tsp vanilla extract
- 50g chocolate chips

 Cooking Time
8 Minutes

 Servings
6

INSTRUCTION

1. In a medium bowl, whisk together the flour, sugar, baking powder, and salt.
2. In another bowl, whisk together the milk, egg, melted butter, and vanilla extract until well combined.
3. Add the wet ingredients to the dry ingredients and mix until just combined. Do not overmix.
4. Fold in the chocolate chips.
5. Lightly grease the air fryer basket with cooking spray.
6. Fill a piping bag or a ziplock bag with the batter and cut a small hole in one corner.
7. Pipe the batter into the air fryer basket, making 4-6 donuts depending on the size of your basket.
8. Air fry at 180°C for 6-8 minutes or until the donuts are golden brown and a toothpick inserted in the center comes out clean.
9. Let the donuts cool in the basket for 5 minutes before removing them.

Birthday Cake Donuts

INGREDIENTS

- 200g plain flour
- 80g caster sugar
- 1 tsp baking powder
- 1/2 tsp bicarbonate of soda
- 1/2 tsp salt
- 120ml buttermilk
- 2 large eggs
- 2 tbsp unsalted butter, melted
- 1 tsp vanilla extract
- 50g rainbow sprinkles

For the glaze:
- 125g icing sugar
- 1 tbsp milk
- 1/2 tsp vanilla extract
- More sprinkles for decoration

INSTRUCTION

1. In a large mixing bowl, whisk together the flour, sugar, baking powder, bicarbonate of soda, and salt.
2. In a separate bowl, whisk together the buttermilk, eggs, melted butter, and vanilla extract.
3. Add the wet ingredients to the dry ingredients and mix until just combined. Fold in the sprinkles.
4. Transfer the batter to a piping bag or a ziplock bag with a corner snipped off.
5. Pipe the batter into the donut molds in the air fryer basket, filling each mold about 2/3 full.
6. Cook the donuts in the air fryer at 180°C for 6-8 minutes or until lightly golden and springy to the touch.
7. Allow the donuts to cool in the mold for a few minutes before transferring them to a wire rack to cool completely.
8. To make the glaze, whisk together the icing sugar, milk, and vanilla extract in a small bowl until smooth.
9. Dip each donut into the glaze, allowing the excess to drip off. Sprinkle additional rainbow sprinkles on top.
10. Allow the glaze to set for 10-15 minutes before serving.

 Cooking Time 8 Minutes   **Servings** 12

Caramel Donuts

INGREDIENTS

- 250g self-raising flour
- 80g caster sugar
- 1 large egg
- 125ml milk
- 2 tbsp vegetable oil
- 1 tsp vanilla extract
- 4 tbsp caramel sauce
- 50g unsalted butter, melted
- 100g icing sugar
- 2 tbsp milk

 Cooking Time
10 Minutes

 Servings
12

INSTRUCTION

1. In a large bowl, whisk together the flour and caster sugar.
2. In a separate bowl, beat the egg and mix in the milk, vegetable oil, and vanilla extract.
3. Pour the wet mixture into the dry mixture and stir until well combined.
4. Fold in the caramel sauce.
5. Spoon the mixture into a piping bag and pipe into a greased donut pan.
6. Place the donut pan into the air fryer and cook at 180°C for 8-10 minutes.
7. Once cooked, remove the donuts from the pan and brush with melted butter.
8. In a bowl, whisk together the icing sugar and milk until a smooth glaze forms.
9. Dip the donuts into the glaze and allow to set for 5-10 minutes before serving.

Blueberry Donuts

INGREDIENTS

- 125g all-purpose flour
- 1 tsp baking powder
- 1/4 tsp baking soda
- 1/4 tsp salt
- 50g granulated sugar
- 1 egg
- 70ml buttermilk
- 2 tbsp melted butter
- 1/2 tsp vanilla extract
- 50g fresh blueberries

For the glaze:

- 80g icing sugar
- 1-2 tbsp milk
- 1/4 tsp vanilla extract

 **Cooking Time
10 Minutes** **Servings
6**

INSTRUCTION

1. In a bowl, mix together the flour, baking powder, baking soda, salt, and sugar.
2. In another bowl, whisk the egg, buttermilk, melted butter, and vanilla extract.
3. Add the wet ingredients to the dry ingredients and mix until just combined. Fold in the blueberries.
4. Spoon the batter into a piping bag or ziplock bag with a corner snipped off.
5. Pipe the batter into the donut molds of your air fryer. Make sure to only fill them about 2/3 of the way.
6. Air fry at 180°C for 8-10 minutes or until the donuts are golden brown and cooked through.
7. Meanwhile, make the glaze by whisking together the icing sugar, milk, and vanilla extract.
8. Once the donuts are done, let them cool for a few minutes before dipping them into the glaze.
9. Place the glazed donuts on a wire rack to set.

Chai Spiced Donuts

INGREDIENTS

- 180g all-purpose flour
- 50g granulated sugar
- 2 tsp baking powder
- 1/2 tsp salt
- 1 tsp ground cinnamon
- 1/2 tsp ground ginger
- 1/4 tsp ground cardamom
- 1/4 tsp ground nutmeg
- 1/4 tsp ground cloves
- 120ml milk
- 1 egg
- 1 tsp vanilla extract
- 2 tbsp melted butter
- Cooking spray

For the glaze:
- 125g powdered sugar
- 2 tbsp milk
- 1/2 tsp vanilla extract
- 1/4 tsp ground cinnamon
- 1/8 tsp ground ginger
- 1/8 tsp ground cardamom
- Pinch of salt

INSTRUCTION

1. In a mixing bowl, whisk together the flour, sugar, baking powder, salt, and spices.
2. In a separate bowl, whisk together the milk, egg, vanilla extract, and melted butter.
3. Add the wet ingredients to the dry ingredients and stir until just combined.
4. Lightly spray the air fryer basket with cooking spray.
5. Spoon the batter into a piping bag or a large plastic bag with the corner snipped off.
6. Pipe the batter into the air fryer basket, filling each donut mold about 2/3 full.
7. Air fry at 180°C for 8-10 minutes, until the donuts are golden brown and cooked through.
8. Remove the donuts from the air fryer and let them cool for a few minutes.
9. While the donuts are cooling, make the glaze by whisking together the powdered sugar, milk, vanilla extract, spices, and salt until smooth.
10. Dip the cooled donuts into the glaze, shaking off any excess.
11. Place the glazed donuts on a wire rack to set for a few minutes.

 Cooking Time
10 Minutes

 Servings
6-8

Matcha Donuts

 Cooking Time
10 Minutes

 Servings
6-8

INGREDIENTS

- 150g all-purpose flour
- 30g cornstarch
- 2 teaspoons baking powder
- 1/4 teaspoon salt
- 1 tablespoon matcha powder
- 100g granulated sugar
- 1 large egg
- 120ml milk
- 2 tablespoons vegetable oil
- 1/2 teaspoon vanilla extract

For the glaze:
- 75g powdered sugar
- 1 tablespoon milk
- 1/2 teaspoon matcha powder

INSTRUCTION

1. In a large bowl, whisk together the flour, cornstarch, baking powder, salt, matcha powder, and sugar.
2. In a separate bowl, whisk together the egg, milk, vegetable oil, and vanilla extract.
3. Add the wet ingredients to the dry ingredients and mix until just combined.
4. Spoon the batter into a piping bag or a plastic bag with a small corner cut off.
5. Pipe the batter into a preheated air fryer donut mold, filling each mold about 2/3 full.
6. Cook in the air fryer at 180°C for 8-10 minutes, or until the donuts are lightly browned and spring back when touched.
7. While the donuts are cooking, make the glaze by whisking together the powdered sugar, milk, and matcha powder until smooth.
8. Once the donuts are done cooking, let them cool in the mold for a few minutes before removing them.
9. Dip the cooled donuts into the glaze, turning to coat all sides.
10. Let the glaze set for a few minutes before serving. Enjoy your delicious matcha donuts!

Peanut Butter & Jelly Donuts

INGREDIENTS

- 180g all-purpose flour
- 70g granulated sugar
- 2 tsp baking powder
- 1/2 tsp salt
- 120ml milk
- 60g creamy peanut butter
- 1 egg
- 1 tsp vanilla extract
- 60ml vegetable oil
- 4 tbsp strawberry jelly or jam
- 60g powdered sugar
- 1-2 tbsp milk

INSTRUCTION

 Cooking Time
10 Minutes

 Servings
6

1. In a medium bowl, whisk together the flour, granulated sugar, baking powder, and salt.
2. In a separate bowl, whisk together the milk, peanut butter, egg, and vanilla extract until well combined.
3. Pour the wet ingredients into the dry ingredients and mix until just combined. Do not overmix.
4. Use a piping bag or a spoon to fill the donut molds of the air fryer with the batter.
5. Cook the donuts in the air fryer at 180°C for 8-10 minutes, until golden brown.
6. Allow the donuts to cool slightly before removing them from the molds.
7. Once the donuts have cooled completely, fill a piping bag with the strawberry jelly or jam. Insert the tip of the piping bag into each donut and fill it with the jelly or jam.
8. In a small bowl, whisk together the powdered sugar and 1 tablespoon of milk. Add more milk as needed to create a thick glaze.
9. Dip the tops of the donuts into the glaze and place them on a wire rack to dry.
10. Allow the glaze to set for 10-15 minutes before serving.

Lemon Poppy Seed Donuts

 **Cooking Time** 10 Minutes   **Servings** 6-8

INGREDIENTS

- 140g all-purpose flour
- 50g granulated sugar
- 1 tbsp poppy seeds
- 1 tsp baking powder
- 1/4 tsp baking soda
- 1/4 tsp salt
- 1 large egg
- 75ml buttermilk
- 40ml vegetable oil
- 1 tsp vanilla extract
- Zest of 1 lemon

For the glaze:
- 100g icing sugar
- 2-3 tbsp lemon juice

INSTRUCTION

1. In a mixing bowl, whisk together the flour, sugar, poppy seeds, baking powder, baking soda, and salt.
2. In another bowl, beat the egg and then whisk in the buttermilk, vegetable oil, vanilla extract, and lemon zest.
3. Pour the wet ingredients into the dry ingredients and mix until just combined. Be careful not to overmix.
4. Transfer the batter to a piping bag or a ziplock bag with one corner snipped off.
5. Pipe the batter into the donut molds in the air fryer basket, filling each mold about 2/3 of the way full.
6. Cook the donuts in the air fryer at 180°C for 8-10 minutes, or until they are lightly golden brown and a toothpick inserted in the center comes out clean.
7. While the donuts are cooking, prepare the glaze by whisking together the icing sugar and lemon juice until smooth.
8. When the donuts are done, remove them from the air fryer basket and let them cool for a few minutes.
9. Dip the top of each donut in the glaze and then let them sit for a few minutes to allow the glaze to set.

Churro Donuts

INGREDIENTS

- 120g all-purpose flour
- 1/4 tsp baking powder
- 1/4 tsp baking soda
- 1/4 tsp salt
- 1/2 tsp cinnamon
- 60g unsalted butter, melted
- 50g granulated sugar
- 1 large egg
- 1 tsp vanilla extract
- 80ml milk
- 80g sugar + 1 tsp cinnamon (for coating)
- Cooking spray

INSTRUCTION

1. In a bowl, mix together the flour, baking powder, baking soda, salt, and cinnamon until combined.
2. In another bowl, mix together the melted butter and granulated sugar until well combined.
3. Add the egg and vanilla extract to the butter-sugar mixture and mix well.
4. Gradually add the flour mixture and milk to the butter-sugar mixture, alternating between the two, and mix until the batter is smooth.
5. Grease the air fryer basket with cooking spray.
6. Spoon the batter into a piping bag or a plastic bag with the tip cut off.
7. Pipe the batter into the air fryer basket in a circular shape to form a donut. Repeat until all the batter is used up, leaving some space in between each donut.
8. Air fry at 180°C for 8-10 minutes or until the donuts are golden brown and fully cooked.
9. While the donuts are still warm, mix together the sugar and cinnamon for the coating in a shallow bowl.
10. Dip each donut in the sugar-cinnamon mixture until fully coated.
11. Serve warm and enjoy!

 Cooking Time
10 Minutes

 Servings
6

Carrot Cake Donuts

 **Cooking Time** 10 Minutes

 Servings 6

INGREDIENTS

- 150g all-purpose flour
- 50g whole wheat flour
- 1/4 teaspoon baking soda
- 1 teaspoon baking powder
- 1/2 teaspoon ground cinnamon
- 1/4 teaspoon ground ginger
- 1/4 teaspoon ground nutmeg
- 1/4 teaspoon salt
- 2 medium carrots, grated
- 60ml vegetable oil
- 75g brown sugar
- 1 large egg
- 60ml milk
- 1/2 teaspoon vanilla extract
- 30 g chopped walnuts

For the glaze:

- 60g cream cheese, softened
- 3 tablespoons powdered sugar
- 1/2 teaspoon vanilla extract
- 1 tablespoon milk

INSTRUCTION

1. In a medium bowl, whisk together the all-purpose flour, whole wheat flour, baking soda, baking powder, cinnamon, ginger, nutmeg, and salt.
2. In a separate bowl, combine the grated carrots, vegetable oil, brown sugar, egg, milk, and vanilla extract. Mix until well combined.
3. Add the wet ingredients to the dry ingredients and mix until just combined. Do not overmix.
4. Fold in the chopped walnuts.
5. Spoon the batter into a piping bag fitted with a large round tip.
6. Pipe the batter into a greased donut pan, filling each mold about 3/4 full.
7. Preheat the air fryer at 180°C for 5 minutes.
8. Place the donut pan into the air fryer and cook for 8-10 minutes until golden brown.
9. Remove the donut pan from the air fryer and let cool in the pan for a few minutes before removing them and placing them on a wire rack to cool completely.
10. To make the glaze, whisk together the cream cheese, powdered sugar, vanilla extract, and milk until smooth.
11. Drizzle the glaze over the cooled donuts and serve.

Raspberry Donuts

INGREDIENTS

- 150g all-purpose flour
- 50g granulated sugar
- 1 tsp baking powder
- 1/4 tsp baking soda
- 1/4 tsp salt
- 1/2 tsp ground cinnamon
- 120ml buttermilk
- 1 large egg
- 1/2 tsp vanilla extract
- 2 tbsp unsalted butter, melted
- 80-100g fresh raspberries
- 2 tbsp raspberry jam
- 30g powdered sugar, for dusting

 Cooking Time 10 Minutes   **Servings** 4-6

INSTRUCTION

1. In a large mixing bowl, whisk together the flour, granulated sugar, baking powder, baking soda, salt, and cinnamon.
2. In a separate bowl, whisk together the buttermilk, egg, and vanilla extract. Add the melted butter and whisk until well combined.
3. Pour the wet ingredients into the dry ingredients and stir until just combined. Gently fold in the fresh raspberries and raspberry jam.
4. Spoon the batter into a piping bag fitted with a medium-sized round tip.
5. Lightly spray the air fryer basket with cooking spray. Pipe the batter into the basket to form 4-6 donuts.
6. Air fry at 180°C for 8-10 minutes, or until the donuts are lightly golden brown and a toothpick inserted into the center comes out clean.
7. Carefully remove the donuts from the air fryer and transfer them to a wire rack to cool.
8. Once the donuts have cooled, dust them with powdered sugar and serve.

Banana Bread Donuts

INGREDIENTS

- 2 ripe bananas, mashed
- 50g granulated sugar
- 50g light brown sugar
- 60ml vegetable oil
- 1 large egg
- 1/2 tsp vanilla extract
- 120g all-purpose flour
- 1 tsp baking powder
- 1/2 tsp baking soda
- 1/2 tsp ground cinnamon
- 1/4 tsp salt
- Optional: chopped walnuts, for topping

INSTRUCTION

1. In a mixing bowl, combine the mashed bananas, granulated sugar, brown sugar, vegetable oil, egg, and vanilla extract. Mix until smooth.
2. In a separate bowl, whisk together the flour, baking powder, baking soda, cinnamon, and salt.
3. Add the dry ingredients to the banana mixture and stir until just combined.
4. Spoon the batter into a piping bag or a zip-top bag with a corner snipped off.
5. Pipe the batter into the donut mold of your air fryer, filling each mold about 2/3 full.
6. Top with chopped walnuts, if desired.
7. Air fry at 180°C for 8-10 minutes, or until the donuts are golden brown and a toothpick inserted into the center comes out clean.
8. Let cool for a few minutes before removing from the molds.
9. Serve and enjoy!

 Cooking Time
10 Minutes

 Servings
4-6

Cranberry Orange Donuts

INGREDIENTS

- 125 g all-purpose flour
- 100 g granulated sugar
- 1 tsp baking powder
- 1/2 tsp salt
- 60 ml unsalted butter, melted
- 120 ml buttermilk
- 1 egg
- 75 g dried cranberries
- 1 tbsp orange zest
- 75 g powdered sugar
- 1 1/2 tbsp orange juice

INSTRUCTION

1. In a mixing bowl, combine the flour, sugar, baking powder, and salt.
2. In a separate bowl, whisk the melted butter, buttermilk, and egg until well combined.
3. Pour the wet ingredients into the dry ingredients and mix until smooth.
4. Fold in the dried cranberries and orange zest.
5. Using a piping bag or ziplock bag with one corner snipped off, pipe the batter into 6 donut molds.
6. Place the molds into the air fryer basket and cook at 180°C for 8-10 minutes or until a toothpick comes out clean.
7. Remove the molds from the air fryer and let the donuts cool for 5 minutes before removing them from the molds.
8. In a small bowl, whisk together the powdered sugar and orange juice until smooth.
9. Drizzle the glaze over the cooled donuts and let it set before serving.

 Cooking Time
10 Minutes   **Servings**
6

Apple Crisp/Crumble

INGREDIENTS

- 3 large apples, peeled, cored, and sliced
- 50g caster sugar
- 50g plain flour
- 50g rolled oats
- 50g unsalted butter, chilled and cut into small pieces
- 1 tsp ground cinnamon
- 1/4 tsp ground nutmeg
- 1/4 tsp salt

 Cooking Time 20 Minutes   **Servings** 4

INSTRUCTION

1. In a mixing bowl, combine the sliced apples with the caster sugar, cinnamon, nutmeg, and salt. Toss until the apples are coated.
2. In a separate bowl, mix together the flour, rolled oats, and butter until the mixture resembles coarse breadcrumbs.
3. Layer the sliced apples in the bottom of an air fryer-safe baking dish.
4. Sprinkle the crumble mixture evenly over the apples.
5. Place the baking dish in the air fryer basket and cook at 180°C for 15-20 minutes, or until the topping is golden brown and the apples are tender.
6. Serve hot with a dollop of whipped cream or ice cream on top.
7. Enjoy your delicious Apple Crisp/Crumble made in the air fryer!

Sticky Toffee Pudding

Cooking Time 20 Minutes

Servings 4-6

INGREDIENTS

- 175g pitted dates, chopped
- 175ml boiling water
- 1 tsp bicarbonate of soda
- 75g unsalted butter, at room temperature
- 175g caster sugar
- 2 large eggs
- 175g self-raising flour
- 1 tsp vanilla extract
- 150ml double cream
- 50g dark muscovado sugar
- 25g unsalted butter

INSTRUCTION

1. In a bowl, combine the chopped dates, boiling water, and bicarbonate of soda. Let it sit for 10 minutes to soften the dates.
2. In a separate bowl, cream together the unsalted butter and caster sugar until light and fluffy. Beat in the eggs one at a time.
3. Sift in the self-raising flour and fold until combined. Stir in the vanilla extract.
4. Fold in the date mixture and mix until everything is evenly distributed.
5. Grease a 6-inch cake tin that fits in your air fryer with butter. Pour in the cake mixture and smooth out the top.
6. Put the tin in the air fryer and cook at 160°C for 20 minutes. Check the cake with a skewer — it should come out clean when inserted into the middle. If it needs more time, cook for a further 5 minutes at a time until it's cooked.
7. While the cake is cooking, make the toffee sauce. Heat the double cream, dark muscovado sugar, and unsalted butter in a small saucepan over medium heat, stirring until the sugar dissolves.
8. Bring to a boil and cook for 2-3 minutes until the sauce thickens.
9. Once the cake is cooked, remove it from the air fryer and let it cool for a few minutes. Pour the toffee sauce over the cake and serve while still warm.

Bread Pudding

INGREDIENTS

- 400g stale white bread, crusts removed and cut into cubes
- 600ml whole milk
- 3 large eggs
- 100g granulated sugar
- 1 tsp ground cinnamon
- 1 tsp vanilla extract
- 50g raisins or sultanas
- 20g butter, softened

 Cooking Time 30 Minutes   **Servings** 4-6

INSTRUCTION

1. In a large mixing bowl, whisk together the milk, eggs, sugar, cinnamon, and vanilla extract until well combined.
2. Add the cubed bread and raisins/sultanas to the mixture and stir until the bread is fully coated and the raisins/sultanas are evenly distributed.
3. Grease the inside of a baking dish that fits inside your air fryer with the softened butter.
4. Pour the bread pudding mixture into the greased baking dish and smooth out the top.
5. Place the baking dish inside the air fryer basket and cook at 160°C for 25-30 minutes, or until the top is golden brown and the pudding is cooked through.
6. Carefully remove the baking dish from the air fryer and allow it to cool for a few minutes before serving.

Lemon Tart

INGREDIENTS

- 200g plain flour
- 100g butter, chilled and diced
- 1 egg yolk
- 1 tablespoon cold water
- 3 large eggs
- 125ml double cream
- 125ml freshly squeezed lemon juice
- 100g caster sugar
- Zest of 1 lemon

 Cooking Time
30 Minutes

 Servings
6

INSTRUCTION

1. In a large mixing bowl, combine the flour and butter. Rub the butter into the flour using your fingers until the mixture resembles breadcrumbs.
2. Add the egg yolk and cold water to the bowl and mix with a fork until a dough forms.
3. Knead the dough on a lightly floured surface until smooth, then wrap in clingfilm and chill for 30 minutes.
4. Preheat the air fryer to 180°C.
5. Roll out the chilled pastry on a lightly floured surface to a thickness of about 3mm.
6. Use the pastry to line a 20cm tart tin, trimming any excess.
7. Prick the base of the pastry with a fork and line with baking paper and baking beans.
8. Air fry the pastry case for 8 minutes, then remove the baking beans and paper and air fry for a further 5 minutes until lightly golden.
9. In a separate bowl, whisk together the eggs, double cream, lemon juice, caster sugar and lemon zest.
10. Pour the mixture into the pastry case and air fry for 15-20 minutes until the filling is set and lightly golden.
11. Remove from the air fryer and allow to cool before slicing and serving.

Scones

INGREDIENTS

- 225g self-raising flour
- 50g unsalted butter, chilled and cubed
- 25g caster sugar
- 150ml milk
- 1 egg, beaten
- Pinch of salt
- Jam and clotted cream, to serve

 Cooking Time
10 Minutes

 Servings
6

INSTRUCTION

1. In a large mixing bowl, combine the self-raising flour and salt. Rub in the chilled butter until the mixture resembles breadcrumbs.
2. Stir in the caster sugar and gradually add in the milk, mixing until the dough comes together. Be careful not to overmix.
3. On a lightly floured surface, roll out the dough to about 2cm thickness. Use a scone cutter to cut out the scones and place them on a baking sheet lined with parchment paper.
4. Brush the scones with beaten egg and place them in the air fryer basket, making sure to leave enough space for air to circulate.
5. Cook the scones in the air fryer at 180°C for 8-10 minutes or until golden brown and cooked through.
6. Serve the scones warm with jam and clotted cream.

Custard Tart

INGREDIENTS

- 1 sheet of shortcrust pastry
- 240 ml of milk
- 120 ml of heavy cream
- 100g of sugar
- 3 egg yolks
- 1 teaspoon of vanilla extract
- 1/4 teaspoon of salt
- Ground nutmeg

 Cooking Time
20 Minutes

 Servings
6-8

INSTRUCTION

1. Roll out the shortcrust pastry and cut it into circles to fit your air fryer tart pan. Gently press the pastry into the tart pan and trim off any excess pastry.
2. In a saucepan, heat the milk and heavy cream over low heat. Add the sugar, egg yolks, vanilla extract, and salt. Whisk until combined and continue to cook over low heat, stirring constantly until the custard thickens.
3. Once the custard has thickened, remove it from the heat and allow it to cool.
4. Pour the cooled custard into the prepared tart shell and smooth out the surface. Sprinkle the top of the tart with ground nutmeg.
5. Place the tart into the air fryer basket and set the temperature to 175°C. Cook for 15-20 minutes or until the pastry is golden brown.
6. Once the tart is cooked, remove it from the air fryer and allow it to cool before serving.

Bakewell Tart

INGREDIENTS

- 175g self-raising flour
- 75g unsalted butter, chilled and diced
- 25g caster sugar
- 1 medium egg, beaten
- 1 tsp cold water
- 4 tbsp raspberry jam
- 100g ground almonds
- 100g caster sugar
- 2 medium eggs, beaten
- 1 tsp almond extract
- 25g flaked almonds

 Cooking Time 30 Minutes **Servings** 6-8

INSTRUCTION

1. In a mixing bowl, combine the flour and chilled butter. Rub the mixture together with your fingertips until it resembles fine breadcrumbs.
2. Stir in the caster sugar and make a well in the centre. Add the beaten egg and cold water and stir to form a soft dough.
3. Knead the dough lightly on a floured surface, then roll it out to fit an 18cm round flan dish. Prick the base of the pastry with a fork and chill in the fridge for 10-15 minutes.
4. Spread the raspberry jam over the base of the pastry case.
5. In a separate mixing bowl, combine the ground almonds, caster sugar, beaten eggs, and almond extract. Mix well.
6. Pour the mixture into the pastry case over the jam and smooth the surface.
7. Sprinkle the flaked almonds over the top of the mixture.
8. Place the tart in the air fryer basket and cook at 160°C for 25-30 minutes or until the pastry is golden brown and the filling is set.
9. Remove from the air fryer and allow to cool before serving. Enjoy!

Fruit Skewers with Yogurt Dip

INGREDIENTS

- 200g Greek yogurt
- 2 tbsp honey
- 1 tsp vanilla extract
- 1 small pineapple, peeled, cored, and cut into chunks
- 1 small watermelon, cut into chunks
- 2 mangoes, peeled and cut into chunks
- 1 punnet of strawberries, hulled
- 12 skewers

 Cooking Time
7 Minutes

 Servings
4-6

INSTRUCTION

1. In a small bowl, mix together the Greek yogurt, honey, and vanilla extract until well combined. Set aside.
2. Thread the fruit onto the skewers in any order you like.
3. Preheat your air fryer to 180°C.
4. Place the fruit skewers in the air fryer basket and cook for 5-7 minutes or until the fruit is slightly caramelized.
5. Serve the fruit skewers with the yogurt dip on the side.

Cinnamon Roll

INGREDIENTS

- 500g bread flour
- 7g fast action yeast
- 75g caster sugar
- 1 tsp salt
- 1 egg
- 250ml milk
- 75g butter, softened
- 50g brown sugar
- 2 tbsp ground cinnamon
- 2 tbsp butter, melted

For the Icing:

- 100g icing sugar
- 2 tbsp milk

 Cooking Time 12 Minutes   **Servings** 6

INSTRUCTION

1. In a large bowl, mix together the flour, yeast, caster sugar, and salt.
2. In a separate bowl, whisk together the egg and milk, then add it to the dry ingredients. Mix until a dough forms.
3. Knead the dough on a floured surface for 10 minutes, then place it in a greased bowl and cover with a damp tea towel. Let the dough rise in a warm place for an hour.
4. Roll out the dough on a floured surface to form a rectangle.
5. In a small bowl, mix together the brown sugar and cinnamon.
6. Spread the softened butter evenly over the dough, then sprinkle the cinnamon sugar mixture on top.
7. Starting from the longer edge, roll up the dough tightly into a log. Cut into 12 even slices.
8. Place the slices in the air fryer basket and brush each one with melted butter.
9. Air fry the cinnamon rolls at 160°C for 10-12 minutes, until they are golden brown and cooked through.
10. While the cinnamon rolls are cooling, make the icing. Whisk together the icing sugar and milk until smooth.
11. Drizzle the icing over the cooled cinnamon rolls and serve.

Printed in Great Britain
by Amazon